NEW INSIGHTS
INTO THE
Old
Testament

NEW INSIGHTS
INTO THE
Old
Testament

ALLAN K. BURGESS

BOOKCRAFT
SALT LAKE CITY, UTAH

Library of Congress Catalog Card Number: 93-73839
ISBN 0-88494-907-9

First Printing, 1993

Printed in the United States of America

Contents

Preface

Contained within the pages of the Old Testament are tremendous stories of faith and courage that reveal God's love for his children and the great lengths to which he will go to help them gain eternal life. As we study God's dealings with these people, we can gain significant insights that will help us solve the problems we face in our lives. Although the people of the Old Testament lived thousands of years ago, they faced the same kinds of moral and spiritual difficulties that we struggle with. Cain's killing of his brother for personal gain could be taken from today's headlines. Enoch's willingness to accept a call in spite of handicaps is duplicated daily by hundreds of faithful members of the Church. As we read about Joseph's resolution to maintain his chastity in the face of an almost overwhelming barrage of temptation, we find ourselves examining our own moral standards and recommitting ourselves to a life of chastity. Samson's failure to live up to his foreordination causes each of us to contemplate our own lives and the things we are doing to help build the kingdom of God. Contained in the Old Testament are stories of action and romance, loyalty and friendship, faith and hardship, courage and commitment. Each of these stories teaches us something about ourselves and our relationship with God.

This book was written for but one purpose—to help members of the Church come to better understand and live the gospel of Jesus Christ. Each chapter not only examines and clarifies certain Old Testament stories and writings but also discusses how these concepts and teachings can be applied in our lives today. God explained to the Prophet Joseph Smith that Abraham, Isaac, and Jacob "have entered into their exaltation . . . and sit upon thrones, and are not angels but are gods" (D&C 132:37). As we study their lives and the lives of other Old Testament prophets—and endeavor to keep the Lord's commandments as they did—we will draw close to our Father in Heaven and become eligible to receive the blessings that they received.

1

And They Shall Be One Flesh

GENESIS 2–3

MOSES 3–4

After Adam had been created and placed in the Garden of Eden, God declared that it was not good for man to be alone and said that he would make a help meet for Adam. The animals and birds were created and placed on the earth, but there still "was not found an help meet for" Adam. (See Genesis 2:18–20.)

As we come to understand what the term *meet* means, we better perceive the proper role between husband and wife. A help meet for Adam was a person who was suited to or worthy of or corresponding to Adam. Eve was equal to him, and together they became a perfect fit, a complete whole.

When we understand the greatness of Adam, we comprehend the majesty of Eve. Adam was known as Michael in the pre-existence and stands next to Jesus in priesthood authority and importance. Adam is the archangel, or chief angel, and as such all other angels were and are under his direction.

Under Jesus' direction, Adam led the armies of heaven in casting out the rebellious Lucifer and his followers. He will also lead the last great battle against Satan, which will take place at the end of the Millennium. Adam will sound his trump to begin the resurrection of the dead (see D&C 29:26).

When we consider that Eve was a perfect match for Adam, we realize how righteous and stalwart she must have been. Both of them came to realize that they were partners in a great work.

God stressed the importance of the marriage bond when he said, "Therefore shall a man leave his father and his mother, and shall cleave unto his wife: and they shall be one flesh" (Genesis 2:24). Next to our relationship with God, there is no relationship as important as the one between husband and wife. President Benson said: "There are only two commandments where the Lord tells us to love someone with all our hearts. The first you are familiar with as the Great Commandment: 'Thou shalt love the Lord thy God with all thy heart, and with all thy soul, and with all thy mind.' (Matt. 22:37.) The second commandment to love one another with all our hearts is this: 'Thou shalt love thy wife with all thy heart, and shalt *cleave unto her* and none else.' (D&C 42:22.)" (*Ensign,* November 1983, p. 43; italics in original.)

Nothing on this earth should come between a husband and a wife. This includes wealth, possessions, talents, fame, occupations, friends, children, and parents. The Lord has commanded that a husband and wife become one.

The importance of a man leaving his father and his mother and cleaving unto his wife was demonstrated by a newly married couple named Phil and Janece. About eight o'clock on the very first morning of their honeymoon, the phone in their motel room started to ring. When Janece answered the phone, she was surprised to find that it was Phil's mother on the other end of the line. She was calling to give Phil his instructions for the day.

Every evening throughout their honeymoon, Phil would report to his mother and give her their current phone number, and every morning she would call with new instructions for the next twenty-four hours. This type of relationship continued when Phil and Janece returned home, except that Phil's mother began to instruct Janece as well. She would tell her what to cook for the day and even make sure that she had the recipes that Phil was used to.

The mother's constant meddling in her son's marriage

caused a lot of friction and kept Phil and Janece from developing the important relationship they needed as husband and wife. Within a few weeks the couple separated. They might have enjoyed a happy and successful marriage if Phil had only been willing to leave his parents and cleave unto his wife.

Talking about newlyweds, President Spencer W. Kimball counseled, "Your married life should become independent of her folks and his folks. You love them more than ever; you cherish their counsel; you appreciate their association; but you live your own lives, being governed by your decisions, by your own prayerful considerations after you have received the counsel from those who should give it." (*Ensign,* March 1977, p. 5.)

Following the fall of Adam and Eve, God taught another great concept about the marriage relationship. The Lord explained one of the consequences of the fall to Eve by saying, "I will greatly multiply thy sorrow and thy conception; in sorrow thou shalt bring forth children; and thy desire shall be to thy husband, and he shall rule over thee" (Genesis 3:16).

President Kimball helped us understand this scripture:

> The Lord said to the woman: ". . . in sorrow thou shalt bring forth children." I wonder if those who translated the Bible might have used the term *distress* instead of sorrow. It would mean much the same, except I think there is great gladness in most Latter-day Saint homes when there is to be a child there. As He concludes this statement he says, "and thy desire shall be to thy husband, and he shall rule over thee." . . . It [the word *rule*] gives the wrong impression. I would prefer to use the word *preside* because that's what he does. A righteous husband presides over his wife and family. ("The Blessings and Responsibilities of Womanhood," *Ensign,* March 1976, p. 72.)

Every unit of the Church is presided over by someone who has been called by and is responsible to the Lord. Because the family is the most important unit in the Church, the Lord has designated someone to preside over it. Generally, this is the father of the family. In section 121 of the Doctrine and Covenants, God explains the only acceptable way for fathers and all priesthood leaders to preside:

No power or influence can or ought to be maintained by virtue of the priesthood, only by persuasion, by long-suffering, by gentleness and meekness, and by love unfeigned;

By kindness, and pure knowledge, which shall greatly enlarge the soul without hypocrisy, and without guile. . . .

Let thy bowels also be full of charity, . . . and let virtue garnish thy thoughts unceasingly. (D&C 121:41–42, 45.)

When God said to Eve, "Thy desire shall be to thy husband," he wasn't talking about something forced that would take place against her will. He was identifying feelings that would spring out of respect and love. It is not difficult to believe that Adam was the kind of man who followed the Lord's counsel and treated his wife as an equal. Because he never forced or demanded but led with love, kindness, and patience, Eve's natural desire would be to follow Adam. She would know that he was in tune with God and would respond willingly.

The Apostle Paul explained this loving, trusting relationship between husbands and wives when he said,

Wives, submit yourselves unto your own husbands, as unto the Lord.

For the husband is the head of the wife, even as Christ is the head of the church: and he is the saviour of the body.

Therefore as the church is subject unto Christ, so let the wives be to their own husbands in every thing.

Husbands, love your wives, even as Christ also loved the church, and gave himself for it. (Ephesians 5:22–25.)

No faithful woman resents Christ presiding over the Church, because she knows that Christ loves her and has sacrificed in her behalf. When a husband loves his wife as Christ loves us, it is natural for his wife to desire to follow him. When a husband unselfishly sacrifices for his wife as Christ did for us, it is easy for a wife to respond to his leadership. After all, she knows that he has her best interests in mind. When a husband treats his wife with love and respect and includes her in the decision-making process, husband and wife grow closer together and find it easier to fulfill their marriage roles.

2

And They Did Eat

GENESIS 3

Because Satan knew not the mind of God (Moses 4:6), he sought to get Adam and Eve to partake of the forbidden fruit—the fruit of the tree of the knowledge of good and evil. Some enticements that he used with Adam and Eve are still being tried on us today.

Satan's initial approach to Eve is an interesting one. He said, "Yea, hath God said, Ye shall not eat of every tree of the garden?" (Genesis 3:1.) This was true as far as it went, but Satan conveniently failed to mention the last part of God's statement, which was "But of the tree of the knowledge of good and evil, thou shall not eat of it" (Genesis 2:17). Satan works in the realm of rationalizations and half-truths. He sprinkles truths among his lies in order to make his temptations seem more enticing and appealing. He hopes that partial truths will give his lies more credibility.

Eve didn't fall for this particular half-truth and said to him, "We may eat of the fruit of the trees of the garden: but of the fruit of the tree which is in the midst of the garden, God hath said, Ye shall not eat of it, neither shall ye touch it, lest ye die." (Genesis 3:2–3.)

The commandment to not even touch the fruit is instructional. One of the best ways to avoid sin is to refrain from any contact with it. We will never read a questionable book if we never pick it up, and unwholesome magazines will not find their way into our lives if they never find a way into our hands.

Satan then followed with another half-truth. "Ye shall not surely die: for God doth know that in the day ye eat thereof, then your eyes shall be opened, and ye shall be as gods, knowing good and evil." (Genesis 3:4–5.)

This argument enticed Eve to take a closer look at the tree and its fruit. What happened next is an almost perfect pattern for many of the sins that are committed today. The scriptures say, "When the woman saw that the tree was good for food, and that it was pleasant to the eyes, and a tree to be desired to make one wise, she took of the fruit thereof, and did eat, and gave also unto her husband with her; and he did eat" (Genesis 3:6).

This process might have happened quickly or might have taken quite some time, but the same six steps that Eve followed are emulated by many in our day:

1. The fruit on the tree looked good.
2. The more Eve looked at it, the more pleasant it became to her eyes.
3. She continued to look at the fruit until she desired it.
4. Her desire led her to finally pick the fruit and hold it in her hand.
5. Once the fruit was in her hand, it wasn't long until she partook of it. (Maybe just one small bite at first to see if it really tasted as good as it looked.)
6. She then got her husband to eat of the fruit.

The scriptures say that when they partook of the fruit, "the eyes of them both were opened, and they knew that they were naked" (Genesis 3:7). Before they partook of the fruit they were innocent, but now they had a clearer understanding of right and wrong—they had received knowledge of good and evil. Because of the circumstances, partaking the fruit was not considered a sin but was referred to as a transgression. Joseph Fielding Smith said, "When [Adam] ate, he became subject to death, and therefore he became mortal. This was a transgression of the law, but not a sin in the strict sense, for it was something that Adam and Eve had to do!" (*Doctrines of Salvation*, comp. Bruce R. McConkie [Salt Lake City: Bookcraft, 1954], 1:115.)

Adam and Eve must not have considered it a sin, for after learning of the atonement of Christ, they actually rejoiced at the consequences of their actions. Adam said, "Blessed be the name of God, for because of my transgression my eyes are opened, and in this life I shall have joy, and again in the flesh I shall see God." Eve rejoiced that, because of their transgression, they had an opportunity to receive joy and eternal life. (Moses 5:10–11.)

Just as children cannot sin before the age of accountability, it is questionable whether Adam and Eve were in a position to truly sin. But they did transgress the law, an act which brought about the Fall and introduced mortality here upon the earth. Not only did Adam and Eve fall from the presence of God, but the whole earth fell also. Brigham Young taught: "When the earth was framed and brought into existence and man was placed upon it, it was near the throne of our Father in heaven. And when man fell . . . the earth fell into space, and took up its abode in this planetary system, and the sun became our light . . . . This is the glory the earth came from, and when it is glorified it will return again unto the presence of the Father, and it will dwell there." (*Journal of Discourses,* 17:143.)

The fall of Adam and Eve, and of this earth, was an important and essential step in God's eternal plan for our progress. Just as Adam and Eve did, we should rejoice because of the Fall. The Fall is a great blessing to us, as it brought about the conditions necessary for true agency and growth. We now have opposition and knowledge, which are both absolutely necessary in the true exercise of agency. And agency is absolutely necessary in our growth toward godhood.

3

And He Became Satan, Even the Devil

JST, GENESIS 3:1–5

MOSES 4:1–4

During our premortal existence, our Heavenly Father presented a plan to us. This plan would give us the opportunity to become like him. One of the most essential ingredients of the plan was the principle of agency. In fact, without the opportunity to freely choose, our growth would be critically limited and the plan would fail.

Because all of us would make incorrect choices, choosing a savior became an essential part of the plan. When God asked "Whom shall I send?" Lucifer said, "Behold, here am I, send me, I will be thy son, and I will redeem all mankind, that one soul shall not be lost, and surely I will do it; wherefore give me thine honor" (Moses 4:1; see also Abraham 3:27).

Lucifer did not want to follow God's plan but wanted to establish a plan of his own. He wanted to take away our agency, a loss which would completely destroy our opportunity of becoming like God. He probably knew that his plan would not work, but his only concern was that he be placed in a position of power and glory.

Jesus, on the other hand, declared, "Father, thy will be done, and the glory be thine forever" (Moses 4:2). Jesus desired no glory for himself but was willing to take upon himself the sins of the world out of love for his Father and for us.

Satan became enraged and led a third part of all the hosts of heaven in an attempt to destroy our agency and, therefore, our future growth and happiness. Concerning this, God told Moses:

> Because that Satan rebelled against me, and sought to destroy the agency of man, which I, the Lord God, had given him, and also, that I should give unto him mine own power; by the power of mine Only Begotten, I caused that he should be cast down;
>
> And he became Satan, yea, even the devil, the father of all lies, to deceive and to blind men, and to lead them captive at his will, even as many as would not hearken unto my voice. (Moses 4:3–4.)

Satan was not cast out of heaven because he disagreed with God but rather because he came out in open rebellion against him. He refused to have anything to do with God and his plan. He wanted total power over everyone, including God.

Referring to Satan and his followers, the Lord revealed to Joseph Smith: "They shall return again to their own place, to enjoy that which they are willing to receive, because they were not willing to enjoy that which they might have received. For what doth it profit a man if a gift is bestowed upon him, and he receive not the gift? Behold, he rejoices not in that which is given unto him, neither rejoices in him who is the giver of the gift." (D&C 88:32–33.)

At least two important lessons can be learned from these scriptures. The first one is that the devil is real and is completely committed to destroying our souls. The war that was started in heaven is still taking place on the earth today. Because we rejected his plan and fought against him, he seeks our total destruction. He delights in those things that cause degradation and misery, and he promotes thoughts and activities that lead to debasement, disgrace, and unhappiness. He is definitely an enemy, and unless we become as totally committed to saving souls as he is to destroying them, we allow him great power.

The scriptures record what overcame Satan in our premortal

existence. These same things will work for us here. The Apostle John described the premortal conflict when he wrote:

> And there was war in heaven: Michael [Adam] and his angels fought against the dragon; and the dragon fought and his angels,
>
> And prevailed not; neither was their place found any more in heaven.
>
> And the great dragon was cast out, that old serpent, called the Devil, and Satan, which deceiveth the whole world: he was cast out into the earth, and his angels were cast out with him. . . .
>
> And they overcame him by the *blood of the lamb,* and by the *word of their testimony*; and they *loved not their lives unto the death.* (Revelation 12:7–9, 11; italics added.)

When we fought face to face with Satan, we realized how dangerous he really was, and therefore we were totally committed to the battle. We need to be just as committed today. Through the Savior's atonement and the great strength that he promises us, and by doing those things that keep our testimonies strong, we can limit the power Satan has in our lives. Eventually, not long after the end of the Millennium, Satan will be completely defeated and will be cast permanently into outer darkness.

The second lesson we can learn is the importance of free agency. We are "free to choose liberty and eternal life, through the great Mediator of all men, or to choose captivity and death, according to the captivity and power of the devil; for he seeketh that all men might be miserable like unto himself" (2 Nephi 2:27).

As we contemplate the war that was fought in heaven to secure our agency, it should bring to our minds the importance of allowing those around us their agency. Sometimes, in the name of love, we try to force or coerce others into doing things that we feel are right.

Such was the case with Virginia. She had married a man who was not active in the Church. He smoked and drank and had other vices that she did not like, but she felt that, because she loved him and he loved her, he would soon give these vices up and take her to the temple to be sealed to him. For twenty years she pushed and shoved and tried to coerce her husband into becoming religious, but to no avail. As a matter of fact, because of her constant badgering, he had built up a resistance against the Church. To him it had become a matter of pride, and he felt that he would be losing face if he gave in to her demands and changed his ways.

Virginia became so frustrated and unhappy that she sought the advice of her bishop. She told him that her life was miserable and that she was constantly bickering with her husband. She felt that her situation was no longer bearable.

Her bishop told her that she really only had three options: (1) she could leave her husband and live alone; (2) she could continue on her present course of being miserable unless her husband changed and met her expectations; (3) she could accept and love her husband for what he was and give him the freedom and space to make his own decisions. If she chose this third option, she could not constantly worry about how to get him to change but would concentrate on being a better wife and a happier person.

After giving these three options a lot of thought and prayer, Virginia decided to accept her husband for what he was and give him the freedom to make his own decisions. Within just a few years, her husband decided to become active in the Church, and it wasn't long after that until they were sealed in the temple.

Love, kindness, unselfishness, generosity, testimony, faith, and all other godly qualities are never developed through force. They are developed through the proper use of agency. That is why God told us that no righteous influence can be maintained through compulsion or control but only through persuasion, long-suffering, meekness, kindness, and love (see D&C 121:37–42). We can encourage and support others in such a way that they know we care and yet they realize that their spiritual growth is totally their responsibility. As we do this, we will be following God's plan—which is the only plan that really works.

4

I Know Not, Save the Lord Commanded Me

JST, GENESIS 4

MOSES 5:1–12

After Adam and Eve were driven from the garden, they had sons and daughters, who in turn began "to divide two and two in the land." Adam and Eve became grandparents as their own children "begat sons and daughters." (Moses 5:3.)

Adam and Eve continued to be faithful and call upon the name of the Lord. Even though they were shut out from his presence, they heard his voice and responded to it. About this time, one of the most inspiring events in all of scripture took place.

They had been commanded by God to offer the firstlings of their flocks as an offering to him, and they had faithfully obeyed this commandment. One day an angel of the Lord appeared to Adam and said, "Why dost thou offer sacrifices unto the Lord? And Adam said unto him: I know not, save the Lord commanded me." (Moses 5:6.)

The immense love, obedience, and trust that Adam and Eve felt for the Lord was clearly revealed in this simple statement. They had been cast out of the garden and been cut off from the

Lord's presence, yet they had been faithful and obedient and had continued to serve him. It appears that up to this time they had not been taught the full plan of salvation and the gift of repentance, yet their trust in God was complete. Even though they did not realize they could be forgiven and live with God again, they still obeyed him faithfully. This obedience must have come from a deep and profound love for their Heavenly Father.

"And then the angel spake, saying: This thing [the offering of the firstlings of their flocks] is a similitude of the sacrifice of the Only Begotten of the Father, which is full of grace and truth." The angel told them that everything they did should be done in the name of the Son, and he advised them to "repent and call upon God . . . forevermore." The Holy Ghost came upon Adam and Eve and, after bearing record of the Savior, said, "As thou hast fallen thou mayest be redeemed, and all mankind, even as many as will." (Moses 5:7–9.)

Notice the great joy that filled the souls of Adam and Eve as they were taught the gospel and came to understand that they could be forgiven and live with God again. When Adam heard these things he blessed God and was filled with the Spirit, exclaiming "Blessed be the name of God, for because of my transgression my eyes are opened, and in this life I shall have joy, and again in the flesh I shall see God." Eve was equally happy, for she said, "Were it not for our transgression we never should have had seed, and never should have known good and evil, and the joy of our redemption, and the eternal life which God giveth unto all the obedient." (Moses 5:10–11.)

The great joy that obedience brought to the lives of Adam and Eve can be part of our lives also as we respond to God's teachings and direction. We can trust him enough that we do not need to know why he wants us to do something before we can obediently serve him.

One twelve-year-old boy told his father that he would start living the law of the fast if his dad could give him one good reason to do so. When his father talked about the money that was given to the poor through fasting, the boy replied that the family could afford to eat and still donate to the poor. The father then suggested that fasting brought a person closer to God, but the boy indicated that hunger was the only feeling he felt when he fasted. Every reason his father came up with was repudiated by the young man. Finally the father turned to the scriptures. After reading about Adam's faithful obedience, they turned to Isaiah in the Old Testament and read, "For my thoughts are not your thoughts, neither are your ways my ways, saith the Lord. For as the heavens are higher than the earth, so are my ways higher than your ways, and my thoughts than your thoughts." (Isaiah 55:8–9.)

The father explained that, since God is a lot smarter than us, sometimes our obedience should be based not on under-standing but on trust. Through the power of the Holy Ghost, this important message was carried to the heart and mind of this twelve-year-old boy, and from that moment on he has faith-fully lived the law of the fast. More important, he has come to trust the Lord in all areas of his life, realizing that God sees much further down the road than he does.

Elder Heber J. Grant declared, "No amount of knowledge, no amount of testimony, no amount of sealing in the temples of God to our wives and children will save us; but the keeping of the commandments of God, being honest in our dealings with God and with our fellow men, paying our tithing, obeying the Word of Wisdom and doing our duty as Latter-day Saints—these are the things, and the only things that will save us" (Conference Report, October 1900, p. 60).

Obedience is the key that unlocks and makes available the blessings of heaven. "When we obtain any blessing from God, it is by obedience to that law upon which it is predicated" (D&C 130:21). Obedience also develops character. As we obey our Father in Heaven, one of the greatest blessings we receive is that we become more like him. And the ultimate reason for us being here is that we might cultivate and acquire for ourselves the same character traits as God.

5

Cain Loved Satan More Than God

GENESIS 4

MOSES 5

Having learned about the plan of salvation and the Atonement, Adam and Eve enthusiastically taught the gospel to their sons and daughters, but it appears that their children rejected the word of God. The scripture says that "Satan came among them, saying: I am also a son of God; and he commanded them, saying: Believe it not; and they believed it not, and they loved Satan more than God." (Moses 5:13.)

Adam and Eve continued to call upon God, and eventually Cain was born. Hoping that Cain would respond to the gospel, Eve declared, "I have gotten a man from the Lord; wherefore he may not reject his words." As Cain grew older, her hopes were crushed; "Cain hearkened not" to the word of God but said, "Who is the Lord that I should know him?" (Moses 5:16.)

Finally, however, a righteous son was born to Adam and Eve. They named him Abel, and how they must have rejoiced when he desired to serve the Lord! Realizing the potential for good that Abel represented, Satan moved quickly to have his influence removed.

Satan commanded Cain to make an offering to the Lord, and Cain responded to his command. Instead of bringing a lamb to the altar, which represented the Lamb of God being slain for the sins of the world, Cain made an offering of the fruit of the ground. His offering was rejected for two reasons: it was performed incorrectly, and his motives were evil. When God rejected the offering, Cain became very angry, but the Lord said, "If thou doest well, thou shalt be accepted. And if thou doest not well, sin lieth at the door." (Genesis 4:7.)

What a great lesson for us! We need to accept responsibility for our own actions and not blame others or God when wrong choices lead to negative consequences.

As Abel grew he continued to walk in holiness before the Lord, but Cain listened no more to God's teachings. This brought great heartache to Adam and Eve, who mourned deeply because of the wickedness of Cain and their other children.

Cain and some of his brothers became so wicked that they made a pact with Satan. "Satan said unto Cain: Swear unto me by thy throat, and if thou tell it thou shalt die; and swear thy brethren by their heads, and by the living God, that they tell it not; for if they tell it, they shall surely die; and this that thy father may not know it; and this day I will deliver thy brother Abel into thine hands. And Satan sware unto Cain that he would do according to his commands. And all these things were done in secret." (Moses 5:29–30.)

Cain was so evil that he said, "Truly I am Mahan, the master of this great secret, that I may murder and get gain. . . . And he gloried in his wickedness." After killing his brother, "Cain gloried in that which he had done, saying: I am free; surely the flocks of my brother falleth into my hands." (Moses 5:31–33.)

The nearsightedness of his sin soon became apparent, for, just five verses later, Cain declared, "My punishment is greater than I can bear" (Moses 5:38).

Cain's agreement with Satan to "murder and get gain" was the first of many secret combinations that have existed upon the earth. Since that time, literally millions of people have suffered because of these combinations. When people combine the desire to gain money or power with the willingness to commit evil deeds and then bind themselves together by an oath to accomplish their designs, a secret combination is formed.

Secret combinations destroyed both the Nephite and the Jaredite civilizations. While the Nephites were concentrating on their external enemy, the Lamanites, a more dangerous enemy gained power from within. These secret combinations, fed by personal greed and materialism, eventually led to the total destruction of the Nephite nation.

In the book of Ether, Moroni warned us to beware of secret combinations in our day. He said, "Whatsoever nation shall uphold such secret combinations, to get power and gain, until they shall spread over the nation, behold, they shall be destroyed" (Ether 8:22).

If we recognize that secret combinations often seek wealth or power through the abuse of others, we can easily identify many of them in today's world. Drug cartels, cigarette manufacturers, beer and liquor companies, and numerous other organizations put personal profit ahead of the health and welfare of others. Greed, not concern for others, becomes the overriding consideration.

Sometimes we think of secret combinations as large organizations and overlook the fact that just one person and the devil may constitute a secret combination. As soon as someone makes the decision to get money or power through dishonesty and makes an evil covenant to do so, he or she loves Satan more than God and forms a secret combination. These combinations usually start small and grow by degrees until people do things that formerly they never would have dreamed of doing.

One man made the decision to gain money through fraud. When it looked as if his scheme was going to be discovered, he placed a bomb in a business associate's driveway in order to divert attention and suspicion from himself. The associate's wife picked up the package containing the bomb and was killed. When asked if he felt bad about killing the wrong person, the man explained that he hadn't really cared who picked up the bomb. Apparently it could have been children from next door as far as he was concerned. The purpose of the bomb would still have been fulfilled. This secret combination consisted of Satan and just one man, yet it caused a great deal of pain and heartache.

Another man, who was professionally involved in the stock market, decided to tamper with a pharmaceutical company's product and laced its medicine with poison. Because of his foreknowledge that the drug would have to be removed from store shelves, this man made a big profit on the company's stock. It didn't seem to matter to the man that a totally innocent woman died from taking the drug.

As in these two examples, some secret combinations consist of just one person and Satan. Therefore it is important for us to carefully examine our own lives and identify any tendencies we might have that Satan might try to exploit. None of us has reached the level of these two examples, but do we seek in any way to gain power or money through dishonest means? Do we take credit for the work of others in order to move up in our job? Do we cheat on our income tax? Are we keeping secrets from our spouse or our bishop because we are ashamed of some of the things we are doing? Is greed, materialism, or a desire to get ahead at the expense of another creeping into our thoughts or actions?

Jacob, a Book of Mormon prophet, said: "Think of your brethren like unto yourselves, and be familiar with all and free with your substance, that they may be rich like unto you. But before ye seek for riches, seek ye for the kingdom of God." (Jacob 2:17–18.)

Jacob's message is clear. God wants us to place him first in our lives. As we replace pride, greed, and materialism with humility, generosity, and charity, God will make us truly rich by blessing us with the blessings of eternity. In a revelation given to Joseph Smith and Oliver Cowdery, the Lord said, "Seek not for riches but for wisdom, and behold, the mysteries of God shall be unfolded unto you, and then shall you be made rich. Behold, he that hath eternal life is rich." (D&C 6:7.)

Jacob indicated that, after we have gained a hope in Christ by seeking and obtaining the mysteries of God and the riches of eternity, if we desire to help the poor and the needy, God will help us because our hearts are right. He will also help us in our struggle to overcome feelings of greed and selfishness if we will but invite him into our hearts through sincere prayer and honest effort. Then we will become combined with God rather than Satan and will help rather than hinder those we come in contact with. Instead of saying, "My punishment is greater than I can bear," we will be able to say, "My soul was filled with exceedingly great joy."

6

And Enoch Walked with God

JST, GENESIS 6–7

MOSES 6–7

All of us are spirit children of God, yet many times we feel inadequate when Church callings are presented to us. We feel that we lack faith, or don't have the ability to succeed, or have circumstances in our lives that will keep us from fulfilling the call. Enoch suffered from some of these same feelings.

One day, as Enoch was traveling, the Spirit of God descended upon him and he heard a voice from heaven, saying: "Enoch, my son, prophesy unto this people, and say unto them—Repent, for thus saith the Lord: I am angry with this people, and my fierce anger is kindled against them; for their hearts have waxed hard, and their ears are dull of hearing, and their eyes cannot see afar off." (Moses 6:26–27.)

The people to whom Enoch was being called to preach repentance would not be considered golden contacts. They had denied God and sought their own counsels. They had deliberately broken the commandments and had devised murders in order to get gain. They had formed secret combinations and sworn oaths of secrecy. Greed and selfishness had become paramount in their lives. In God's own words, "They have brought upon themselves [spiritual] death; and a hell I have prepared for them, if they repent not." (Moses 6:28–29.)

Probably none of us would be too excited about accepting this particular call, but Enoch faced other problems besides the wickedness of the people. Enoch said, "Why is it that I have found favor in thy sight, and am but a lad, and all the people hate me; for I am slow of speech; wherefore am I thy servant?" (Moses 6:31.)

Enoch might have felt young and slow of speech, but he had one strength that is vital in our service to the Lord—he was truly humble. He also must have had a great trust and faith in God because, in spite of the people's wickedness and his own weaknesses, he accepted the call. These people had mocked and rejected him because of his speech, yet he had enough trust in the Lord to ignore this past ridicule and face these same people head on, even calling them to repentance.

All of us can receive inspiration and spiritual strength from this account of Enoch. With the Lord's help, Enoch became a powerful preacher and leader and helped bring people to repentance and establish a city of righteousness—Zion.

Every promise that the Lord made Enoch came to pass. The Lord said to Enoch, "Go forth and do as I have commanded thee, and no man shall pierce thee." Since many of his hearers were murderers, this was a significant promise. The scriptures indicate that when Enoch testified against their works, "all men were offended because of him," yet no harm came to him. When they heard him, "no man laid hands on him; for fear came on all them that heard him; for he walked with God." (Moses 6:32–39.)

In response to his slowness of speech, God promised, "Open thy mouth, and it shall be filled, and I will give thee utterance, for all flesh is in my hands, and I will do as seemeth me good." Enoch's speech became powerful; indeed, some of the greatest teachings of all scripture are found in the writings of Enoch. As Enoch preached the word of God, "the people trembled, and could not stand in his presence." (Moses 6:32, 47.)

God told Enoch that his Spirit was upon him and that mountains would flee before him and rivers would turn from their courses. When enemies came to battle against the people of God, Enoch "spake the word of the Lord, and the earth trembled, and the mountains fled, even according to his command; and the rivers of water were turned out of their course; . . . and all nations feared greatly, so powerful was the word of Enoch, and so great was the power of the language which God had given him" (Moses 7:13). Remember that these mighty miracles were performed by a man who had been hated and ridiculed because of his speech.

God promised Enoch, "Thou shalt abide in me, and I in you" and then gave him the inspiring invitation, "Walk with me" (Moses 6:34). Enoch did walk with God and received great blessings because of it. This same promise is available to all of us. God desires to walk with us and will do so as long as our feet are on his path. Every Church calling that we receive is accompanied by the promise that God will abide with us if we will do our best.

The people had hardened their hearts and could not see "afar off," but Enoch was told that if he anointed his eyes with clay and washed them, he would be able to see (see Moses 6:27, 35). When he did so, he was shown all things from the beginning of the world to the end, including such events as the atonement of the Savior, the restoration of the priesthood in the latter days, the second coming of Christ, and the return of the city of Zion to the earth. Because he was able to see things that were not visible to the natural eye, he was called a seer. We have seers today who are able to "see afar off" and help us prepare for the future. Each general conference we sustain the President of the Church and the Apostles as prophets, seers, and revelators.

Fashioning a Zion out of the society that Enoch lived in was an incredible accomplishment. Of those remaining on earth after Zion was taken to heaven, God told Enoch, "Among all the workmanship of mine hands there has not been so great wickedness as among thy brethren" (Moses 7:36). Out of this kind of situation Enoch taught and led a people that became "of one heart and one mind, and dwelt in righteousness; and there was no poor among them" (Moses 7:18). This kind of leadership came from a relatively young man who had at one time been rejected and ridiculed.

Enoch is a perfect example of what can happen when we

allow the Lord to "walk with us." Many so-called average men and women have become some of the greatest leaders in the world as they have lived the gospel and responded to the Lord. Joseph Smith received little formal schooling, yet he developed from a farm boy to one of the greatest leaders of all time.

Brigham Young was an expert carpenter when he joined the Church. Through service in the kingdom, he developed into a powerful leader who led thousands of Saints across the plains and directed the settling of hundreds of colonies throughout the West. God expanded and refined Brigham's skills and talents as he served faithfully in the Church.

John Taylor was a turner and Heber C. Kimball a potter when they joined the Church. The Church gave them an opportunity to strengthen their characters and expand their leadership abilities.

Mary Fielding Smith is an example of a faithful woman who overcame great opposition and, through her great courage and devotion, inspired thousands of Church members to live better lives.

The transforming power of the gospel is available to all. As we receive opportunities to serve and encounter obstacles to overcome, with the help of the Lord our talents and capacities will increase accordingly. When we receive calls to serve that seem overwhelming to us, we can remember Enoch and Joseph and Mary and realize that the Lord will help us also. He has promised us that he will prepare a way for us to accomplish anything he asks us to do and that he will keep his promises to us just as he did with Enoch. And, as with Enoch, he will walk with us as we strive to do his will.

7

Enoch's Heart Swelled Wide as Eternity

JST, GENESIS 7

MOSES 7:26–69

A bishop received an unusual phone call. When he picked up the phone, a voice on the other end said, "You don't know me and you will probably think this is a joke, but something evil is taking over my mind and I need help."

Because there was such a tone of sincerity and fear in the voice, the bishop knew the caller was serious and told him to meet him at his office immediately. When the caller arrived, he was a young man, wild in appearance and definitely in a state of panic.

The young man, who was named Rick, told the bishop a truly frightening story. He was not a member of the Church but had been taught good Christian principles in his home. During the last few years of his life, Rick had violated everything good that his parents had taught him. He said that he had felt especially troubled by an unseen power for several weeks, but the potency of this power had increased many-fold during the past few hours. That morning at work, Rick had began seeing people as if it were through someone else's eyes. He seemed to know the evil thoughts and desires of those he worked with. With the desperate realization that he was losing his identity to some outside power, he had run to a phone booth located near his office.

Rick had felt that he had just one chance—to talk to a man of God. He had turned to the yellow pages where churches were listed and started calling from the top of the list. The bishop was the first "minister" to answer his phone.

The bishop explained that because of Rick's disregard for the ways of God, he was rapidly succumbing to the devil's power. He told Rick that he could give him a blessing that would solve the present crisis, but that a permanent solution was in his hands only, depending on whether he corrected his life to conform with the will of God. Accordingly a blessing was given, the evil spirit was cast out, and Rick was promised that he would have peace of mind long enough to sort out his life and make some important decisions.

Rick requested that the bishop teach him about the gospel, and when he left he took several Church books with him. That night Rick called the bishop when it started to get dark—he was afraid that the "something" would come back again. He received assurance from the bishop that everything would be all right and hung up the phone with relief.

The next morning, the bishop contacted the stake missionaries and gave them Rick's name and address. Two or three weeks later, Rick called the bishop again. This time he sounded completely different. Confidence had replaced fear, and happiness had engulfed his previous pain. He sounded enthusiastic and happy as he told how he had gained a personal testimony of the gospel. Rick was going to be baptized the following Saturday, and he wanted the bishop to perform the baptism.

Following the baptism, as Rick and the bishop sat alone in the dressing room, Rick told about the great change that had taken place in his life. As tears rolled down their cheeks, they bore sacred testimony to each other.

Since that time Rick has served a faithful mission, married in the temple, and become a righteous patriarch of an eternal family. Rick's experience illustrates a very important truth: There are two forces that can influence and guide our lives. As we fill our lives with thoughts and actions that are sponsored by

Satan, we fall more and more under his influence. As we do the things the Lord desires of us, we receive more and more help from him.

We receive wages from whomever we decide to obey. The wages for serving God include guidance, comfort, happiness, peace, and a fulness of joy in the celestial kingdom. God has promised us that everything he has will be ours if we will but follow him.

Some are deceived by Satan's counterfeits and decide to follow him instead of God. Satan rewards his loyal followers with momentary pleasure but also with pain, suffering, depression, and unhappiness. Satan has no worthwhile reward to offer for obedience to him, and even if he did, he wouldn't make it available to his followers.

God's goal is to help us obtain lasting happiness. Satan, on the other hand, desires to make us miserable like himself. A great comparison between God's motives and Satan's is found in Moses 7. Enoch was shown a vision that included the people at the time of Noah. Notice Satan's feelings for these people who had loyally done the things he had prompted them to do: "And [Enoch] beheld Satan; and he had a great chain in his hand, and it veiled the whole face of the earth with darkness; and he looked up and laughed, and his angels rejoiced" (Moses 7:26).

When Enoch saw that Satan rejoiced in such things as child abuse, cruelty, murder, immorality, and all types of vulgarity and profanity, his desire to avoid Satan and the things that he promulgates must have intensified.

Enoch also came to realize the way God felt about the people at Noah's time: "And it came to pass that the God of heaven looked upon the residue of the people, and he wept: and Enoch bore record of it, saying: How is it that the heavens weep, and shed forth their tears as the rain upon the mountains?" (Moses 7:28.)

God replied: "Wherefore, I can stretch forth mine hands and hold all the creatures which I have made; and mine eye can pierce them also, and among all the workmanship of mine hands there has not been so great wickedness as among thy brethren. But behold, their sins shall be upon the heads of their fathers; Satan shall be their father, and misery shall be their doom; and the whole heavens shall weep over them, even all the workmanship of mine hands; wherefore should not the heavens weep, seeing these shall suffer?" (Moses 7:36–37.)

One purpose of this revelation may have been to help Enoch expand his vision of the importance of each soul and come to love the people as God did. As wicked as these people were, God still loved them and was weeping because they would have to suffer for their sins.

Enoch's heart was touched and his eternal perspective expanded. The Lord told Enoch "all the doings of the children of men; wherefore Enoch knew, and looked upon their wickedness, and their misery, and wept and stretched forth his arms, and his heart swelled wide as eternity; and his bowels yearned; and all eternity shook" (Moses 7:41).

Enoch—just as God had—began to weep over his brethren and loved them so much that he felt that he could not be comforted. He was then shown the birth and atonement of Christ, and his sorrow turned to rejoicing.

Through these experiences, Enoch came to love even the sinner and to appreciate the great gift of the Atonement. With his expanded love and understanding, he became a mighty force in the hands of the Lord: "Enoch and all his people walked with God, . . . and it came to pass that Zion was not, for God received it up into his own bosom" (Moses 7:69).

Enoch was shown the last days, when another Zion would be established upon the earth. Concerning this Zion, God said: "Truth will I cause to sweep the earth as with a flood, to gather out mine elect from the four quarters of the earth, unto a place which I shall prepare, an Holy City. . . . Then shalt thou and all thy city meet them there, . . . and we will fall upon their necks, and they shall fall upon our necks, and we will kiss each other; and there shall be mine abode . . . and for the space of a thousand years the earth shall rest." (Moses 7:62–64.)

A Zion place is made up of Zion people who establish Zion one person at a time. If each one of us made the decision to become a Zion person and then help our families become Zion families, in time we would be living in Zion communities. President Spencer W. Kimball gave three steps that will help us purify ourselves and become Zion people.

"First, we must eliminate the individual tendency to selfishness. . . . It is incumbent upon us to put away selfishness in our families, our business and professional pursuits, and our Church affairs. Second, we must cooperate completely and work in harmony one with the other." After telling us that the spirit of oneness and cooperation must be present in all that we do, President Kimball quoted the Prophet Joseph Smith, who said, "The greatest temporal and spiritual blessings which always come from faithfulness and concerted effort, never attended individual exertion or enterprise. (*Teachings of the Prophet Joseph Smith,* p. 183.)"

President Kimball continued: "Third, we must lay on the altar and sacrifice whatever is required by the Lord," which begins with a broken heart and a contrite spirit. He said that we must learn what our Church duties are and give them our best efforts, including consecrating our time, talents, and means as dictated by the promptings of the Spirit. "Whether a volunteer, father, home teacher, bishop, or neighbor, whether a visiting teacher, mother, homemaker, or friend—there is ample opportunity to give our all." (See "Becoming the Pure in Heart," *Ensign,* May 1978, p. 81.)

From Adam's time to the present, those individuals who have become Zion people have followed this same pattern. Enoch and his followers were no exception. As we ponder and pray about President Kimball's counsel and then begin applying it in our lives, we will perhaps be hastening the establishment of the latter-day Zion seen by Enoch many thousands of years ago. And we will find that we do not need to wait for the finished product before we feel an increase of peace and happiness. The great thing about the gospel is that the trip can bring great joy long before our desired destination is reached.

8

The Flood—
An Act of Love

GENESIS 6

MOSES 8

Noah was one of the great and noble leaders in the premortal existence. Joseph Smith taught that Noah is Gabriel and stands next to Adam in priesthood authority (see *Teachings of the Prophet Joseph Smith*, p. 157). He was the angel who appeared to Mary and Joseph and announced the birth of our Lord and Savior. What a great honor this must have been! It was certainly much more pleasant than the assignment he filled during his mortal life here upon the earth.

Noah was born into a world filled with sin, yet he and his sons hearkened to the Lord and were called "sons of God." His sons were blessed with daughters, but these daughters rejected the counsel of God and married "sons of men." This displeased God greatly, and he said to Noah, "The daughters of thy sons have sold themselves; for behold mine anger is kindled against the sons of men, for they will not hearken to my voice" (Moses 8:15).

Referring to this verse, Joseph Fielding Smith wrote:

> Because the daughters of Noah married the sons of men
> contrary to the teachings of the Lord, his anger was kindled,

and this offense was one cause that brought to pass the universal flood. . . . The daughters who had been born, evidently under the covenant, and were the daughters of the sons of God, that is to say of those who held the priesthood, were transgressing the commandment of the Lord and were marrying *out of the Church.* Thus they were cutting themselves off from the blessings of the priesthood contrary to the teachings of Noah and the will of God. (*Answers to Gospel Questions,* comp. Joseph Fielding Smith, Jr. [Salt Lake City: Deseret Book Co., 1957], 1:136–37; emphasis in original.)

Talking about marrying out of the Church in our day, President Spencer W. Kimball said:

Religious differences imply wider areas of conflict. Church loyalties and family loyalties clash. Children's lives are often frustrated. The nonmember may be equally brilliant, well trained and attractive, and he or she may have the most pleasing personality, but without a common faith, trouble lies ahead for the marriage. There are some exceptions but the rule is a harsh and unhappy one.

There is no bias nor prejudice in this doctrine. It is a matter of following a certain program to reach a definite goal. (*The Miracle of Forgiveness* [Salt Lake City: Bookcraft, 1969], p. 240.)

When a young man or woman decides to marry out of the Church, he or she also, by necessity, marries out of the temple and, unless a conversion and a temple sealing put things right later, loses the great promise of exaltation and eternal life. They make it much more difficult for both themselves and their children to live the gospel. It is not surprising that prophets have told us that choosing a righteous partner and marrying in the temple may be the most important decision we ever make.

The Lord told Noah that he would give the people a hundred and twenty years to repent, and then, if they did not repent, he would send a flood upon the earth. When Noah approached the people with this news, giants sought to take away his life. These giants were probably warriors who took great pride in their physical prowess and delighted in the shedding of blood. There was a great emphasis on physical attributes and accomplishments in Noah's day, as evidenced by men's reaction to his preaching. After Noah had called on the children of men to repent, they came before him and said, "Are we not eating and drinking, and marrying and giving in marriage? And our wives bear unto us children, and the same are mighty men, which are like unto men of old, men of great renown." (Moses 8:21.) And the people refused to listen to Noah.

This emphasis on the physical seems to prevail in today's world as well. Athletes are revered; physical bodies are tanned, built up, and displayed; and physical strength has become more important than spiritual well-being. As an example, a famous athlete who has a wife and family was arrested for soliciting prostitution. He was able to get out of jail in time to play the second half of a ball game that was scheduled that same evening. When he entered the arena, the crowd rose to its feet and gave him a standing ovation.

This emphasis on the physical over the spiritual is very clearly shown by how people earn their money. An article in *USA Today* discussed some of the sports salaries for a given year and broke them down so they were more understandable (see issue of 5 March 1991, p. 2c). For instance, one basketball player received $1,975 per rebound. Another player received $18,349 per point. A quarterback received $200,000 for every touchdown pass he made, and one boxer received two million dollars for every three-minute round he fought. I compared this to how much schoolteachers in our area made, and I was astounded. We pay millions of dollars to watch athletes perform physical feats, but the people who teach my children receive less than one dollar per student per day.

This is not to suggest that athletics and other physical things are wrong, but rather that the priorities of many have become confused until they feel that physical accomplishments are more important than moral ones.

The people of Noah's time retrogressed from one level to another until "every man was lifted up in the imagination of the thoughts of his heart, being only evil continually" (Moses 8:22), and the earth was filled with violence. In spite of this tremendously evil environment, Noah found grace in the eyes of the

Lord. The scripture says that he was a "just man and perfect in his generations" (Genesis 6:9; Moses 8:27). He and his three sons lived righteous lives and walked with God.

Because of the people's wickedness and because of God's love for all his children, God told Noah, "The end of all flesh is come before me, for the earth is filled with violence, and behold I will destroy all flesh from off the earth" (Moses 8:30).

Because of limited perspective, some have felt that the Flood was an act of cruelty. This could not be further from the truth—the Flood was an act of love. When we make a decision, we do so from the narrow perspective of the present. When God makes a decision, he considers what has happened in the past, what is happening in the present, and what is going to happen in the future. Our decisions usually revolve around us and the few people we associate with. God's decisions take into account those who have lived on the earth, those who now live here, and the unborn spirits that will live on the earth in the future. When God makes a decision, he considers all of his children.

There are at least five groups of people that were affected by the Flood, and all five groups benefited from it. The wicked adults were stopped from their continuous downhill slide into filthiness. Between the time of his death and that of his resurrection, the Savior visited the spirit world and established a program to teach these very people the gospel.

The young children of these wicked people were taken out of their destructive environment, and, as with all children who die before the age of accountability, they became heirs to the celestial kingdom and will receive every blessing that God has to give.

Those people who were righteous between the times of Enoch and Noah were translated and lifted up to join the city of Enoch. Therefore, no righteous people were destroyed in the Flood. (See Moses 7:27.)

The Flood brought a stop to the persecution that Noah and his family had been subjected to; they were then able to start a new society where the Spirit of God was present.

Last of all, the unborn spirits would now be born into a world where they would have a better chance of accepting the gospel and fulfilling the purposes of earth life.

John Taylor summed up the benefits of the Flood well when he said: "Thus justice was satisfied, the law vindicated, the wicked punished, the unborn and pure protected and provided for, and finally, the imprisoned released from their bondage and salvation extended to the prisoners. Was there anything wrong in that. 'Yes,' says the ignoramus who does not know anything about it, 'It was very cruel.' Well, the greatest cruelty there is about such men is that they are cruelly ignorant and do not know what they are talking about." (*Journal of Discourses,* 21:18.)

9

Whose Top May Reach unto Heaven

GENESIS 11:1–9

Many generations after the great flood, most of the people became wicked again and decided to work together to thwart the wishes of God. The historian Flavius Josephus explained some of the motives behind their building the tower of Babel. Here are a few excerpts from his history:

> God admonished them again to send out colonies; but they, imagining the prosperity they enjoyed was not derived from the favour of God, but supposing that their own power was the proper cause of the plentiful condition they were in, did not obey him. . . .
>
> Now it was Nimrod who excited them to such an affront and contempt of God. . . . He persuaded them not to ascribe it to God, as if it was through his means they were happy, but to believe that it was their own courage which procured that happiness. . . . He also said he would be revenged on God, if he should have a mind to drown the world again; for that he would build a tower too high for the waters to be able to reach! and that he would avenge himself on God for destroying their forefathers!

Now the multitude were very ready to follow the determination of Nimrod, and to esteem it a piece of cowardice
to submit to God; and they built a tower, neither sparing
any pains, nor being in any degree negligent about the
work; and, by reason of the multitude of hands employed in
it, it grew very high, sooner than any one could expect. . . .
It was built of burnt brick, cemented together with mortar,
made of bitumen, that it might not be liable to admit water.
(*Antiquities of the Jews,* trans. William Whiston [Grand
Rapids, MI: Kregel Publications, 1960], book 1, 4:1–3.)

Some have taught that the main purpose of the tower of
Babel was to reach into heaven, but Josephus suggested a
much deeper and more wicked motive than this. He claimed
that the people planned on building a tower so high that God
could not kill them with another flood. The implication is that,
once the tower was finished, they felt they could sin without
God being able to stop them. If God caused another flood,
they would simply climb to the top of their tower that reached
"unto the heavens," where they would be safe.

This background is very helpful as we turn to the account of
the tower of Babel in the book of Genesis. Genesis also indi-
cates that their mortar was made from slime, or bitumen, which
was a tarlike substance. The people set their goal for building
the tower, saying, "Let us build us a city and a tower, whose top
may reach unto heaven" (Genesis 11:4). Joseph Smith changed
this to read, "whose top will be high, nigh unto heaven" (JST,
Genesis 11:3).

The key verses in this story are verses 6 and 7: "And the
Lord said, Behold, the people is one, and they have all one language; and this they begin to do: and now nothing will be
restrained from them, which they have imagined to do. Go to,
let us go down, and there confound their language, that they
may not understand one another's speech." (Genesis 11:6–7.)

Think of the wickedness that would take place if nothing
would be restrained that people could imagine. The tower was
to be their place of safety and refuge from the justice and
power of the Lord. No wonder the Lord confounded their language and scattered them abroad!

The idea that we can sin and get away with it has been promoted by Satan since the time of Cain, who said, after killing his brother, "I am free; surely the flocks of my brother falleth into my hands" (Moses 5:33). This soul-destroying doctrine is prevalent in the world today. Talking about the last days, Nephi said: "And there shall be many which shall say: Eat, drink, and be merry; nevertheless, fear God—he will justify in committing a little sin; yea, lie a little, take the advantage of one because of his words, dig a pit for thy neighbor; there is no harm in this; and do all these things, for tomorrow we die; and if it so be that we are guilty, God will beat us with a few stripes, and at last we shall be saved in the kingdom of God. Yea, and there shall be many which shall teach after this manner, false and vain and foolish doctrines." (2 Nephi 28:8–9.)

No one can sin and get away with it—No one! President Spencer W. Kimball said:

> There comes a time when the fornicator, like the murderer, wishes he could hide—hide from all the world, from all the ghosts, and especially his own, but there is no place to hide. There are dark corners and hidden spots and closed cars in which the transgression can be committed, but to totally conceal it is impossible. There is no night so dark, no room so tightly locked, no canyon so closed in, no desert so totally uninhabited that one can find a place to hide from his sins, from himself, or from the Lord. Eventually, one must face the great Maker. (*The Teachings of Spencer W. Kimball*, ed. Edward L. Kimball [Salt Lake City: Bookcraft, 1982], pp. 265–66.)

On the other hand, no one can keep the commandments and not receive the promised blessings. No good deed can be done so anonymously that God does not know about it and reward the doer accordingly. No unselfish act can be performed without receiving the peace and joy that service brings. God is aware of our good desires and efforts and is ready to bless and assist us every step of the way.

10

Abraham Seeks the Blessings of the Priesthood

GENESIS 12

ABRAHAM 1

Since the book of Genesis gives very little information about Abraham as a youth, we are grateful for the writings of Abraham in the Pearl of Great Price. Joseph Smith translated these writings from papyrus found in the catacombs of Egypt.

Abraham was raised in the land of the Chaldeans among people who had turned from the ways of righteousness to the worshiping of heathen gods. In spite of this wicked environment, Abraham grew up desiring to obtain the priesthood of God. Writing about his desires, Abraham said:

> And, finding there was greater happiness and peace and rest for me, I sought for the blessings of the fathers, and the right whereunto I should be ordained to administer the same; having been myself a follower of righteousness, desiring also to be one who possessed great knowledge, and to be a greater follower of righteousness, and to possess a greater knowledge, and to be a father of many nations, a prince of peace, and desiring to receive instructions, and to keep the commandments of God, I became a rightful heir, a

High Priest, holding the right belonging to the fathers (Abraham 1:2).

As we think about Abraham's attitudes and desires, it is important to realize that we usually get what we really desire because we work towards those things. Abraham received the things he desired because he worked for them. His desires can be divided into six different categories.

1. Abraham had received happiness, peace, and rest from living the gospel and now sought for the opportunity to have the priesthood so that he could bring this happiness to others.

2. Even though he was a follower of righteousness, he sought to be an even greater follower of righteousness.

3. Through his righteous living he had received great knowledge, but he desired to receive even greater knowledge. It is very clear that Abraham understood the direct correlation between righteousness and knowledge: "And if a person gains more knowledge and intelligence in this life through his diligence and obedience than another, he will have so much the advantage in the world to come" (D&C 130:19).

4. He desired to be a father of many nations—to have many descendants. The fulfillment of the desire was one of the great promises that God later made to him.

5. Abraham desired to be a prince of peace. He lived in a world of war and conflict yet had received peace and rest from the gospel. He knew of the great peace the gospel could bring and desired to assist others in obtaining this peace by preaching the gospel to them.

6. Although Abraham understood some of the gospel, he desired to receive further instructions and to keep the commandments. He did not desire knowledge in and of itself but rather as a means of being more obedient to God. The more we know, the better we can live; and the better we live, the more we can know.

As Abraham attempted to help his family and friends turn to God, he almost lost his life. In order to understand the circumstances Abraham faced, as well as understand similar Old Testament situations, let's briefly discuss idol worship in ancient days.

Idol worship was much more than the simple worship of

false idols and gods. It included the sacrificing of innocent men, women, and children and revolved around numerous acts of perversion and immorality. Many of those who worshiped idols believed that the gods of nature were aroused by the shedding of blood and through other immoral acts. Many farmers set aside a corner of their fields as a place to worship their gods. This worship would include immorality, in the hope that their gods would cause it to rain on their fields. Many times temples were built and surrounded with groves of trees, in which sexual immorality and perversion took place as part of the religious services. Male and female prostitutes were provided at the temples as part of this worship. Furthermore, babies, children, and virtuous people who would not engage in this sexual immorality were sacrificed in numerous ways to stir up the gods and cause them to pour out blessings upon the people.

Talking about his people, including his father, Abraham wrote: "[They] utterly refused to hearken to my voice; for their hearts were set to do evil, and were wholly turned to the god of Elkenah, and the god of Libnah, and the god of Mahmackrah, and the god of Korash, and the god of Pharaoh, king of Egypt; therefore they turned their hearts to the sacrifice of the heathen in offering up their children unto these dumb idols, and hearkened not unto my voice, but endeavored to take away my life by the hand of the priest of Elkenah." (Abraham 1:5–7.)

Abraham then related that he was to be sacrificed on the same altar on which they had sacrificed men, women, and children in the past. Indeed, three virgins had been offered upon this altar "because of their virtue; they would not bow down to worship gods of wood or of stone," which included accepting everything that went with idol worship.

Just as these three virgins did, Abraham was willing and ready to die for his beliefs—and would have done so had God not intervened.

As the false priests lifted up their hands to kill Abraham on the altar, Abraham lifted up his voice to the Lord. The Lord responded by sending an angel. The angel loosed Abraham's bands, made several promises to him, and told him that he would be led away from his father's land to a land that he knew nothing about. The Lord smote the priest with death, broke down the altar of Elkenah, and destroyed all of the gods of the

land. He then caused a "famine to wax sore in the land of Ur."
(See Abraham 1:15–20, 29–30; 2:1.)

What an inspiration the life of Abraham can be to those
who are raised in less than ideal situations! Abraham was surrounded with perversion and evil—even in his own household,
his father worshiped idols and tried to kill him—yet he sought
and successfully received the blessings and guidance of God.
He didn't waste his time and energy in blaming others for his
situation but took responsibility for his own life and overcame
his situation. As we accept responsibility for our own character
and behavior, we place ourselves in a position to repent and,
with the help of the Lord, take charge of our lives. The seriousness of blaming others for our problems was discussed by Elder
F. Burton Howard:

> Unwillingness to accept the responsibility for and con-
> sequences of one's actions is an all too common condition
> in today's world. Who has not heard of the drunken driver
> who sues his host for allowing him to get drunk, or the acci-
> dent victim who claims damages from the physician who
> tries to help him? Perpetrators of the most heinous crimes
> often plead guilty by reason of insanity or claim that they
> are victims of society's ills. The homeless blame alcohol.
> Alcoholics blame genetic deficiencies. Abusers and adulter-
> ers blame the broken homes of their childhood. And there
> are enough who agree with them to ensure that no one
> need feel terribly guilty for long if they don't want to.
>
> The habit of shifting the burden of guilt onto someone
> else, while perhaps understandable in a secular setting, has
> more serious consequences in a spiritual one. . . .
>
> To excuse misconduct by blaming others is presumptu-
> ous at best and is fatally flawed with regard to spiritual
> things, for "we believe that men will be punished for their
> own sins, and not for Adam's transgression" (Articles of
> Faith 1:2). This not only means that we will not be punished
> for what Adam did in the Garden, but also that we cannot
> excuse our own behavior by pointing a finger to Adam or
> anyone else. The real danger in failing to accept responsibil-
> ity for our own actions is that unless we do, we may never
> even enter on the strait and narrow path. Misconduct that

does not require repentance may be pleasant at first, but it will not be for long. And it will never lead us to eternal life. (*Ensign,* May 1991, pp. 12–13.)

God has told us that we are free to act for ourselves and not be acted upon (see 2 Ne. 2:26). What a great blessing and promise this is, for if we could only become as good as the environment we were born in, we could never become like God. This doctrine brings both freedom and responsibility to each of us—the freedom to act for ourselves and determine our own destiny and the responsibility to account for our actions. With God's help, each of us can overcome the traditions and temptations that pull us down, and can become sons and daughters of Christ.

11

God Establishes a Covenant People

GENESIS 12–17

ABRAHAM 1–2

Many patriarchal blessings indicate that those receiving the blessings are the "seed of Abraham." What does it mean to be the seed of Abraham, and what blessings and responsibilities does it entail? How does a person become the seed of Abraham, and why was circumcision given as a token of the Abrahamic covenant? This chapter will focus on these and other often-asked questions, emphasizing what the covenant of Abraham has to do with us today.

Since Adam's day, from time to time God has chosen a people to teach the gospel and establish his covenants throughout the earth. Before the time of Abraham, the gospel was taught and disseminated by righteous followers of prophets, but around 2000 B.C. Abraham was selected to head a covenant people that would offer the gospel to the rest of the world for all time. God's covenant with Abraham included several promises, but two of them are especially applicable to us as members of The Church of Jesus Christ of Latter-day Saints.

The Lord told Abraham, "Behold, I will lead thee by my hand, and I will take thee, to put upon thee my name, even the

Priesthood of thy father, and my power shall be over thee. As it was with Noah so shall it be with thee; but through thy ministry my name shall be known in the earth forever, for I am thy God." (Abraham 1:18–19.)

What a great promise this is! Before the time of Melchizedek, the priesthood was called "the Holy Priesthood, after the Order of the Son of God" but to avoid the frequent repetition of God's name, the church of that day called the priesthood after Melchizedek, a great high priest (see D&C 107:2–4). Abraham literally took upon himself the name of the Son of God when he received the priesthood.

The last part of this promise implies that the atonement and sacrifice of Christ should be the very center of our teachings, for the Lord said that through the ministry of Abraham and other partakers of the covenant, including Latter-day Saints, his name would be known throughout the earth. Nephi, as a descendent of Abraham, was fulfilling this covenant when he said, "And we talk of Christ, we rejoice in Christ, we preach of Christ, we prophesy of Christ, and we write according to our prophecies, that our children may know to what source they may look for a remission of their sins" (2 Nephi 25:26). No talk, lesson, or testimony should be given without bearing witness of Jesus Christ and the good news of his atonement.

The second promise Abraham received also has a great deal to do with us today. God promised Abraham:

> I know the end from the beginning; therefore my hand shall be over thee.
>
> And I will make of thee a great nation, and I will bless thee above measure, and make thy name great among all nations, and thou shalt be a blessing unto thy seed after thee, that in their hands they shall bear this ministry and Priesthood unto all nations.
>
> And I will bless them through thy name; for as many as receive this Gospel shall be called after thy name, and shall be accounted thy seed, and shall rise up and bless thee, as their father;
>
> And I will bless them that bless thee, and curse them that curse thee; and in thee . . . and in thy seed after thee . . . shall all the families of the earth be blessed, even with the

blessings of the Gospel, which are the blessings of salvation, even of life eternal. (Abraham 2:8–11.)

Although many Latter-day Saints are direct descendants of Abraham, God's chosen people, referred to as the seed of Abraham, are not determined by lineage but by righteousness. Notice that God told Abraham that "as many as receive this Gospel shall be called after thy name, and shall be accounted thy seed, and shall rise up and bless thee, as their father." Those who choose to keep the commandments and are willing to place God first in their lives become known as God's covenant people and as the seed of Abraham.

Circumcision was the unusual sign or token that God instituted in Old Testament times to identify his covenant people. He introduced circumcision by first telling Abraham that the people of God had gone astray and no longer kept the ordinances he had revealed to their fathers. He especially indicated that they did not properly observe "the burial, or baptism" as he had commanded them "but have turned from the commandment, and taken unto themselves the washing of children, and the blood of sprinkling; and have said that the blood of the righteous Abel was shed for sins; and have not known wherein they are accountable before me." (JST, Genesis 17:4–7.)

As these verses point out, the people had lost their understanding of correct gospel principles and had begun to perform incorrect ordinances such as "the washing of children" and "the blood of sprinkling." They performed these ordinances in remembrance of righteous Abel's blood, which they thought had been shed for sins. They misunderstood the fact that, because of the infinite and eternal atonement of Jesus Christ, children under the age of accountability could not sin.

God told Abraham that he was establishing the token of circumcision "that thou mayest know for ever that children are not accountable before me until they are eight years old" (JST, Genesis 17:11). Thus, circumcision became the covenant token, and children were circumcised at eight days old as a reminder that they would become accountable at eight years old and should be baptized at that time. It also reminded parents that their child was born in the covenant and needed to be taught and prepared so that he could make formal covenants with the Lord at the time of his baptism. The following statement adds further light to the token of circumcision:

> The Abrahamic covenant makes frequent reference to one's seed (see Genesis 17:6–12). The organ of the body that produces seed and brings about physical birth is the organ on which the token of the covenant was made. The organ of spiritual rebirth, however, is the heart (see 3 Nephi 9:20). Thus, when a person was circumcised it signified that while he had been born into the covenant, he need not be baptized until he became accountable before the Lord. But spiritual circumcision, or the circumcision of the heart, must take place once one becomes accountable or one is not considered as true Israel. (*Old Testament Student Manual*, p. 69.)

Physical circumcision as a sign of God's covenant people was done away with at the time of Jesus, but the symbolic circumcision of the heart is still in effect. We have a circumcised heart when we love God and desire to keep his commandments. As members of The Church of Jesus Christ of Latter-day Saints, we should have Abraham's covenant as an integral part of our lives, since we promise at baptism that we will serve the Lord by blessing others with the gospel.

The true attitude of a covenant person was illustrated well by a young father named Miguel, who lived in the mountains of Guatemala. He was poor in terms of worldly possessions but rich in testimony and faith. His shirt was ragged, his pants embodied more patches than original material, and he owned no shoes. He had received little formal education, could not read or write, and made less than three hundred dollars a year.

Miguel served as a counselor in the presidency of the small branch in his area. The branch met in a bamboo hut that was deteriorating rapidly, and the roof that sagged just a little bit more each week was stark evidence that the hut would not last much longer.

The missionaries taught a young couple who were preparing for marriage; they were overjoyed when the couple desired to be baptized. The young man and woman desired to be married and baptized the same day, which meant a long bus trip to a neighboring city. The missionaries accompanied the couple and invited Miguel to travel with them. The marriage and the baptism took longer than expected, and when they were ready to leave, the bus that would have returned them home again had already left. They somehow managed to get a ride back to the main road, which only left them a short walk of seventeen miles to their homes.

The couple had some relatives they could stay with, but Miguel needed to get home to his family, so he and the missionaries set out to walk the seventeen miles. After walking for many hours, they came to the steep two-mile climb that would finally bring them home. One of the missionaries was murmuring to himself and asking God why they had to go through this physical torture when he glanced over at Miguel and saw a big smile on his face. After fifteen miles of walking, this missionary could not think of anything to smile about, so he asked Miguel why he was so happy. Miguel's response taught him a great lesson: "I am so happy because we just witnessed two people become members of God's true church." The missionary looked down at Miguel's bare feet, thought of the smile that had lasted for fifteen miles, and, through Miguel, came to realize how wonderful it was to introduce the gospel to others.

Miguel's great joy in sharing the gospel reveals clearly that he is the seed of Abraham. God's promise to Abraham that the gospel would be taken to every nation is being fulfilled by humble men and women like Miguel in every part of the world.

Just a few weeks later, Miguel's devotion was illustrated even further. The bamboo chapel had deteriorated to the point that the last meeting possible was being held there. During the meeting, Miguel stood up and announced that he had been secretly building another chapel for the branch and that it was completed and ready to meet in. Miguel had to work twelve hours a day, six days a week, just to earn a meager living for his family, yet he had devoted nearly every penny he made and all of his extra time during the previous six months to prepare a special meeting place. He had done this on his own simply because of his great love for the Lord and for the members of his branch. Because of his tremendous faith and dedication, the Lord had blessed him so that his family's needs had been taken care of.

As the Lord's covenant people, we have been chosen to spread the good news of Christ throughout the world and to establish the gospel and priesthood in every nation. Just as God promised Abraham that His hand would be over him and that He would bless him without measure, God is with us also. His every wish and desire is to help his children understand and accept the saving principles and ordinances of the gospel. He will bless us with great inspiration, power, and strength as we strive to share the gospel with others.

12

The Sacrifice of Isaac: A Similitude of the Savior

GENESIS 22

Because of his great love for us, God would never ask us to do something painful or even unpleasant unless it would help us in our progression toward eternal life. Opposition, pain, suffering, difficulties, and even temptation are necessary to our spiritual growth, or God would have them removed from us. Because we do not fully understand God's plan for us, many times our obedience has to be based on love, trust, and faith. Such was the case with Abraham. There were many reasons why Abraham could have hesitated when God commanded him to offer up his covenant son on the altar, but he "rose up early" the next morning and proceeded to obey the Lord.

As we discussed in chapter 10, when Abraham was younger he had almost been sacrificed on a pagan altar. God had saved Abraham's life by destroying the altar and killing the false priest. Throughout his life he had been taught of the wickedness of human sacrifice, and now God was asking him to sacrifice his covenant son on an altar. What faith and trust he must have had to still believe in God and faithfully follow this command!

Add to this the fact that only after his parents had waited

and prayed for many years had Isaac been conceived through a miracle of God's, for Sarah had been beyond childbearing age. God had promised Abraham that his descendants would be as the dust of the earth, and that through these descendants all families of the earth would be blessed. The Lord had identified Isaac as the covenant son through whom these blessings would come. Now God required Abraham to kill Isaac.

God not only told Abraham to sacrifice his son but also chose the place where it should take place. God said to Abraham, "Take now thy son, thine only son Isaac, whom thou lovest, and get thee into the land of Moriah; and offer him there for a burnt offering upon one of the mountains which I will tell thee of" (Genesis 22:2).

The land of Moriah was three days' journey away. How Abraham's heart must have ached during those three days! When they reached the spot God had chosen, Abraham had the two young men who had accompanied him wait with the animals, and he and Isaac went into the mountains to "worship."

When they came to the place God had chosen, Abraham built an altar and laid the wood on it. He then bound Isaac and placed him on the altar. But when Abraham raised the knife to slay his son, a voice from heaven called him by name and said, "Lay not thine hand upon the lad, neither do thou any thing unto him: for now I know that thou fearest God, seeing thou hast not withheld thy son, thine only son from me" (Genesis 22:12).

God already knew that Abraham would be totally faithful and obedient to him, for He had earlier said: "Shall I hide from Abraham that thing which I do; seeing that Abraham shall surely become a great and mighty nation, and all the nations of the earth shall be blessed in him? For I know him, that he will command his children and his household after him, and they shall keep the way of the Lord." (Genesis 18:17–19.)

Since God knew that Abraham would obey his command, this experience was for Abraham and Isaac, not for God. There are at least two important reasons why God had Abraham and Isaac suffer the agonizing distress of this experience.

The Prophet Jacob clearly taught that this whole ordeal was "a similitude of God and his Only Begotten Son" (Jacob 4:5).

Abraham was a type of the Father, and, interestingly, his name means "father of a great multitude." Isaac was a type of the Son of God. Isaac's birth—like Jesus'—was miraculous, and, as the Savior later did, Isaac submitted willingly to the will of God. Even the place where Abraham was commanded to sacrifice Isaac was near where Jesus would be crucified some two thousand years later.

The consummate and almost incomprehensible faith of both Abraham and Isaac is described in history written by Flavius Josephus. Although his writings do not carry the same significance as the scriptures, they add interesting insights to the lives of these great men:

> Now Abraham thought that it was not right to disobey God in anything, but that he was obliged to serve him in every circumstance of life. . . . Accordingly, he concealed this command of God, and his own intentions about the slaughter of his son, from his wife, as also from every one of his servants, otherwise he should have been hindered from his obedience to God. . . . On the third day, as soon as he saw the mountain, he left those servants that were with him, . . . and, having his son alone with him, he came to the mountain. It was that mountain upon which king David afterwards built the temple. . . . Now Isaac was twenty-five years old. . . .
>
> As soon as the altar was prepared, and Abraham had laid on the wood, and all things were entirely ready, he said to his son, "O son! I poured out a vast number of prayers that I might have thee for my son; when thou wast come into the world, there was nothing that could contribute to thy support for which I was not greatly solicitous, nor anything wherein I thought myself happier than to see thee grown up to man's estate; . . . but since it was by God's will that I became thy father, and it is now his will that I relinquish thee, bear this consecration to God with a generous mind; for I resign thee up to God, who has thought fit now to require this testimony of honour to himself, on account of the favours he hath conferred on me. . . . Accordingly thou, my son, wilt now die, not in any common way of going out of the world, but sent to God, the Father of all

men, beforehand, by thy own father, in the nature of a sacrifice. . . ."

Now Isaac was of such a generous disposition, as
became the son of such a father, and was pleased with this
discourse, and said, "That he was not worthy to be born at
first, if he should reject the determination of God and of his
father, and should not resign himself up readily to both
their pleasures; since it would have been unjust if he had
not obeyed, even if his father alone had so resolved." So he
went immediately to the altar to be sacrificed. And the
deed had been done if God had not opposed it. (*Antiquities
of the Jews,* trans. William Whiston [Grand Rapids, MI: Kregel Publications, 1960], book 1, 13:2–4.)

This experience must have both deepened and broadened
their understanding of Christ's atonement and caused them to
love and appreciate even more the great eternal sacrifice of the
Father and the Son.

A verse in the Doctrine and Covenants suggests another
reason for Abraham and Isaac facing this test. The members of
the Church in Jackson County had been driven from their
homes during the coldest part of the winter, and their suffering
and despair were severe. The Lord, speaking through Joseph
Smith, said, "Therefore, they must needs be chastened and
tried, even as Abraham, who was commanded to offer up his
only son. For all those who will not endure chastening, but
deny me, cannot be sanctified." (D&C 101:4–5.)

As we overcome obstacles that are placed in our paths, we
develop the spiritual and emotional strength necessary to
receive sanctification and become gods. Both Abraham and
Isaac grew tremendously as they obeyed this difficult commandment. Joseph Smith taught that the knowledge that one's
life is pleasing to God is essential in the development of faith,
and that the only way a person can know that his life is pleasing
to God is to be willing to sacrifice whatever God asks of him
(see *Lectures on Faith* 6:5–8). As Abraham and Isaac left the
mountain that day, they must have felt as never before an overwhelming love and acceptance from God, for they had laid
their all on the Lord's altar.

Talking about the Lord's testing of Abraham, George Q.
Cannon explained:

God did not do this for his own sake for He knew by His foreknowledge what Abraham would do; but the purpose was to impress upon Abraham a lesson and to enable him to attain unto knowledge that he could not obtain in any other way. That is why God tries all of us. . . .

He required Abraham to submit to this trial because He intended to give him glory, exaltation and honor; He intended to make him a king and a priest, to share with Himself the glory, power and dominion which He exercised. (*Gospel Truth,* comp. Jerreld L. Newquist [Salt Lake City: Deseret Press, 1957], 1:113.)

The great faith of Abraham and Isaac is still alive today and can be found in the hearts and lives of thousands of Latter-day Saints. One young naval officer from southeast Asia joined the Church while in the United States, where his government had sent him to receive advanced training. He knew that when he returned home his family would disown him, he would face many social problems, and his military rank would be taken from him. When President Gordon B. Hinckley commented on that great price he had to pay to enjoy the gospel, he responded, "Well, it's true, isn't it? What else matters?" ("It's True, Isn't It?" Brigham Young University Speeches of the Year [Provo, 14 December 1971], p. 1.)

This statement sums up well why each of us should be willing to give whatever is needed for the building of God's kingdom. After all, what else matters? The more we give, the more we grow, and the more we receive in return, until we reach the point that, like Abraham, we too become sanctified. Then, like Abraham and Isaac, we can receive all of the blessings God desires to bestow upon us.

13

And He Loved Her

GENESIS 24

The great prophet and patriarch Abraham understood well the importance of marriage within the covenant. Because he and his family lived among the unbelieving Canaanites, he became deeply concerned about a proper mate for his son Isaac. Abraham had a servant whom he trusted with everything that he owned. In fact, he trusted him enough to have him choose a wife for Isaac. He called the servant to him and said, "Swear by the Lord, the God of heaven, and the God of the earth, that thou shalt not take a wife unto my son of the daughters of the Canaanites, among whom I dwell: but thou shalt go unto my country, and to my kindred, and take a wife unto my son Isaac." (Genesis 24:3–4.)

It is not surprising that the servant had some reservations and questions concerning this assignment. Isaac was about forty years old at this time, and anyone would be concerned about choosing a mate for someone else, especially for another adult. The servant asked Abraham what he should do if the woman he chose would not return with him to Abraham's house. Should he then come back and take Isaac to the woman?

Sensing his servant's lack of confidence, Abraham said, "The Lord God of heaven . . . sware unto me, saying, Unto thy seed will I give this land; he shall send his angel before thee, and thou shalt take a wife unto my son from thence. And if the woman will not be willing to follow thee, then thou shalt be clear from this my oath: only bring not my son thither again." (Genesis 24:7–8.)

The servant, now that he had learned of the promise that an angel would assist him, swore that he would fulfill this assignment and prepared for his journey. He took with him ten camels and left for the city of Nahor in Mesopotamia. Some of these camels carried jewels and other precious things that would be given to the family of the woman chosen for Isaac.

The servant was a righteous man and knew of the importance of choosing a worthy wife for Isaac. Throughout his long journey, he must have pondered and prayed about how to approach this great task. By the time he reached the city, he had formulated a plan.

He had his camels kneel down near a well that was located just outside the city. It was evening, and he knew that many women would soon come to the well to replenish their water supply. With this prayer he put the matter into God's hands:

> O Lord God of my master Abraham, I pray thee, send me good speed this day, and shew kindness unto my master Abraham.
>
> Behold, I stand here by the well of water; and the daughters of the men of the city come out to draw water:
>
> And let it come to pass, that the damsel to whom I shall say, Let down thy pitcher, I pray thee, that I may drink; and she shall say, Drink, and I will give thy camels drink also: let the same be she that thou hast appointed for thy servant Isaac; and thereby shall I know that thou hast shewed kindness unto my master. (Genesis 24:12–14.)

This is quite a test that the servant is asking for. Ten thirsty camels would drink a lot of water, and the wells in those days were either deep pits that a person had to go down into or narrow shafts from which full buckets of water were pulled up with the help of a rope. Either case constituted hard work: to expect a total stranger to volunteer to carry the water for ten thirsty camels was an extraordinary test of character. A woman who would do this would certainly not be afraid of work and would possess many other positive character traits, such as unselfishness, kindness, and a willingness to serve.

About this time, Rebekah, who was a granddaughter of Abraham's brother, came to the well with a pitcher on her shoulder. She was "very fair to look upon, a virgin"; indeed, no man had known any woman "like unto her" (JST, Genesis 24:16).

The servant, surely following the promptings of the Spirit, ran to meet her and asked for a drink from her pitcher. When she was finished giving him a drink, she said, "I will draw water for thy camels also, until they have done drinking" (Genesis 24:19). She then repeatedly filled her pitcher from the well and emptied it into the camels' trough until the thirst of every camel had been satisfied.

The servant gave Rebekah a golden earring and two golden bracelets and asked her who her father was. He also wondered if there was room for his group to stay at her father's house. When she indicated who she was, the servant immediately "bowed down his head, and worshipped the Lord." He thanked the Lord for his great mercy in leading him to the house of his master's brethren. (See Genesis 24:22–27.)

What an important lesson this is for each of us! Many times we pray and ask God for help in our lives but then fail to thank him when the help is received. This immediate heartfelt appreciation displayed by the servant allows us to peek into the soul of a truly humble man.

These events must have seemed quite baffling to Rebekah, for she ran to her house and told her family what she had seen and heard. After listening to Rebekah's story, her brother went out to the well to meet the servant. Not only did the Lord assist the servant but he also inspired Rebekah's family as well. Rebekah's brother told the servant, "Come in, thou blessed of the Lord; wherefore standest thou without? for I have prepared the house, and room for the camels." (Genesis 24:31.)

Food and straw were provided for the camels, and water was furnished so that the servant and the men with him could wash their feet. Then food was placed before them, but Abraham's servant refused to eat until he had explained his errand. His loyalty and obedience to his master were unselfishly placed before his personal desires.

After describing his mission and the events that had taken place at the well, the servant said, "And now if ye will deal kindly and truly with my master, tell me: and if not, tell me; that I may turn to the right hand, or to the left."

Laban, the brother, and Bethuel, the father, then answered, "The thing proceedeth from the Lord. . . . Behold, Rebekah is before thee, take her, and go, and let her be thy master's son's wife, as the Lord hath spoken." (Genesis 24:49–51.)

When Abraham's servant heard these words, "he worshipped the Lord, bowing himself to the earth," and gave the family jewels, clothing, and other precious gifts.

When the servant arose the next morning, he wanted to take Rebekah and leave immediately. Rebekah's brother and mother suggested that she tarry at least ten days, but the servant reminded them that the Lord had been directing him and asked again that they be able to leave immediately. They decided to leave it up to Rebekah. When Rebekah's family said to her, "Wilt thou go with this man?" they were asking a great deal of her. She was to undergo a difficult trip of five hundred miles with men she had known just one day and for the purpose of marrying someone she had never met. She demonstrated great faith and trust in the Lord when she uttered the simple words, "I will go."

Meanwhile, Isaac was playing a difficult waiting game at home. One evening, as he was out in the field meditating, he lifted his eyes toward the horizon and saw the camels coming. There is no doubt that Isaac's faith and trust in the Lord were as strong as Rebekah's. He must have spent not just one evening but many evenings meditating and praying that God would direct the choice of his father's righteous servant.

Like all stories that have God at the helm, the story ends happily. The scripture says, "Isaac brought her into his mother Sarah's tent, and took Rebekah, and she became his wife; and he loved her" (Genesis 24:67.)

Because of the importance of a covenant marriage, we should do as this story illustrates and include God in the decision-making process. There are many people that each of us can come to love, but God will help us choose someone we can be truly happy with.

A few years ago, a man asked a woman named Janie to

marry him. Shortly after they had become engaged, a woman named Anne, whom he had met in the mission field, showed up at his door. When he found that he was attracted to her, yet was engaged to Janie, he became very confused. He finally approached Janie with the problem and told her that he had to make sure that he was doing the right thing. Janie asked him a question that turned out to be an embarrassing one. She said, "Didn't you pray about our engagement before you asked me to marry you?" After he had cleared his throat a few times before answering no, Janie asked an even harder question: "Why didn't you?" The man's answer brought even more embarrassment as he weakly stated, "I didn't think about it."

Janie's questions are important ones. It really is dangerous to make a decision as important as marriage without honestly seeking the Lord's guidance and confirmation. After spending several weeks getting better acquainted with Anne, the young man, to his surprise, realized that he loved both Anne and Janie.

After struggling with his decision for many days, the man found a place where he could communicate with his Father in Heaven without being disturbed. His answer came almost immediately and with much more force than he had expected. Because of the quickness and strength of the answer, this young man realized how important this decision was to God.

A few months later he was married to Janie for time and for all eternity. From the moment that God answered his prayer until today, he has never wondered whether he made a mistake in marrying Janie. His heart is filled with the assurance that their marriage will be a good one as long as they put forth the effort to make it so. What a blessing it has been to both of them to know that their marriage was ordained of God!

Another significant concept can be learned from this account of Isaac and Rebekah. When Rebekah drew water for the ten camels, she showed her true nature. She had no idea that her marriage to a future prophet hung in the balance. As far as she knew, it was just another normal day at the well. That is the way it is with most of us. The kind of person we are is demonstrated daily by how we treat those around us. And the kind of person we are determines the type of people we attract. The key to marrying a great man is to be a great woman, and the key to marrying a noble woman is to be a noble man.

God said, "Intelligence cleaveth unto intelligence; wisdom receiveth wisdom; truth embraceth truth; virtue loveth virtue; light cleaveth unto light" (D&C 88:40). Although this scripture specifically refers to the Resurrection, the principle is very applicable throughout our mortal lives. An important question for each of us to ask ourselves is, "Am I the kind of person who would have offered to draw water for ten thirsty camels?"

14

And He Shall Be Blessed

GENESIS 25–27

The major dissension between the brothers Esau and Jacob revolved around Jacob's receiving the birthright. A brief discussion of the laws that governed birthrights may be helpful in better understanding this and similar Old Testament stories.

Old Testament patriarchs usually governed their families directly. This included wives, unmarried daughters, sons and their families, and so forth. When the patriarch died, he was succeeded as head of the family by one of his sons.

In order to avoid contention, a practice developed of the firstborn son's becoming the new head of the family. He was referred to as the birthright son because, by birth, he received the right to lead the family.

The birthright son became the family's spiritual leader and received a double portion of the father's property. This was to be used to take care of his mother and any unmarried sisters that he might have.

Because many patriarchs had more than one wife, the question arose as to which firstborn son should receive the birthright. Since it was felt that the first wife should have precedence over the other wives, "it was determined that the firstborn son of the first wife would be the birthright son as long as he proved worthy. Only in case of unworthiness or death would the birthright go to the firstborn son of the second wife. No second-born sons were considered for the birthright unless all firstborn sons proved to be unworthy." (Daniel H. Ludlow, "I Have a Question," *Ensign,* September 1980, p. 52.)

Notice that the two main components in determining birthright were righteousness and the order of birth. With this background, let's take a look at the story of Esau and Jacob—a story that troubles many Bible readers.

Isaac was about forty years old when he married Rebekah. As with most Old Testament families, they desired to have children, but Rebekah was barren for about twenty years. After much prayer and earnest pleading with the Lord, Rebekah conceived twins.

When the children "struggled together within her," Rebekah asked the Lord what was happening and why. The Lord told her that two different nations were in her womb and that the older son would serve the younger one.

When Rebekah's delivery day arrived, the first son was red and covered "all over like an hairy garment," so they named him Esau, which means "hairy." The second son was named Jacob, which means "supplanter." This probably alludes to the Lord's statement that Jacob would supplant or take the place of Esau in receiving the birthright.

The boys became men, and Isaac's eyesight became dim as he grew old. One day he told Esau to kill a deer and make a savory meal that he loved, and promised him that he would then bless him.

Rebekah, overhearing this conversation and fearing the birthright was about to be given to the wrong son, decided to deceive Isaac into giving the birthright to Jacob. While Esau was out hunting, she made a meal out of goat meat and told Jacob to take it into his father.

Jacob, foreseeing a problem, said, "Esau my brother is a hairy man, and I am a smooth man" (Genesis 27:11). He knew that if his father were to feel him, he would know that he was not Esau.

Rebekah overcame this problem by dressing Jacob in Esau's clothes and by placing goat skins on Jacob's hands and neck so that he felt hairy instead of smooth. Jacob then took the meal into his father.

Jacob told his father that he was Esau and that he had done as he had been asked. His father felt him and said, "The voice is Jacob's voice, but the hands are the hands of Esau. And he discerned him not, because his hands were hairy, as his brother Esau's hands: so he blessed him." (Genesis 27:22–23.) In this blessing, apparently temporarily forgetting the revelation Rebekah had received when the twins were born, and overlooking the unrighteousness of Esau, Isaac gave the birthright to Esau.

Jacob had no sooner left his father than Esau appeared with his venison meal and requested his blessing. When Isaac realized that Jacob had received the birthright blessing instead of Esau, the Spirit may well have enlarged his spiritual understanding, for he confirmed Jacob's blessing by exclaiming, "Yea, and he shall be blessed."

Some gospel commentators justify Jacob's deception by emphasizing Esau's unworthiness. Others criticize Jacob's deception and feel that Esau should have received the blessing. Both of these approaches leave much to be desired.

A basic understanding of gospel principles and a careful reading of the scriptures clearly lead to the conclusion that Jacob received the birthright blessing, not through deception, but because, in spite of his deception, he was much more righteous than Esau. The birthright was to be conferred upon the firstborn righteous son, and there were several valid reasons why Esau was not worthy to receive it.

1. The Lord had indicated while Jacob and Esau were yet in the womb that the older should serve the younger (see Genesis 25:23).

2. The birthright should have been a treasured thing, yet Esau gave away his birthright for a meal. One day he came in from the field and asked Jacob to feed him with a pottage made from lentils. When Jacob indicated that he would trade him the pottage for his birthright, Esau agreed. Esau even swore a sacred oath to Jacob that the birthright was his, Jacob's. Thus Esau "despised his birthright" and sold it to Jacob in order to satisfy his hunger. Therefore, Esau no longer had the right to seek the birthright (see Genesis 25:29–34).

3. Esau married out of the covenant. When he was forty years old, he married "Judith the daughter of Beeri the Hittite,

and Bashemath the daughter of Elon the Hittite: which were a grief of mind unto Isaac and to Rebekah" (Genesis 26:34–35).

4. Esau was a profane person (see Hebrews 12:16). A profane person shows disregard or contempt for sacred things.

5. Esau's plea to receive the birthright blessing was rejected, for although he "sought it carefully with tears," he was too late, having "despised his birthright" (see Hebrews 12:17; Genesis 25:34).

Clearly the Lord wanted Jacob to receive the birthright; he reaffirmed this many times throughout Jacob's life. Several basic gospel principles also relate to Jacob receiving the birthright. Both of these areas are included in the following ideas that support the legitimacy of Jacob's receiving this blessing.

1. Rebekah knew by personal revelation that Jacob was the birthright son (see Genesis 25:23).

2. The Lord has promised priesthood leaders that whatsoever they bind and loose on earth will take effect in heaven (see Matthew 16:19). Once Isaac realized what had taken place, he could have "loosed" or revoked the blessing and given it to Esau. Instead he indicated that Jacob would retain the blessing (see Genesis 27:33).

3. As soon as Isaac learned what had happened, he affirmed Jacob's right to the birthright blessing (see Genesis 27:33).

4. Isaac called Jacob to him and charged him to leave their home and find a covenant wife among Rebekah's family. Before Jacob left, Isaac asked God to bless him with the covenant blessings of Abraham (see Genesis 28:1–4).

5. Jehovah appeared personally to Jacob and promised him the blessings of Abraham and Isaac. At this time, his name was changed from Jacob to Israel, which means "one who prevails with God" (see Genesis 35:9–12). From that time on, the Lord has used the name Israel to refer to Jacob, to the literal descendants of Jacob, and to all true believers in Christ, regardless of their lineage or geographical location. (See Bible Dictionary: "Israel.")

6. No blessing from the Lord can be received through deceit. "There is a law, irrevocably decreed in heaven before the foundations of the world, upon which all blessings are predicated—and when we obtain any blessing from God, it is by

obedience to that law upon which it is predicated." (D&C 130:20–21.) Jacob did not receive the birthright blessing through his deceit; in spite of this one seemingly unrighteous act, he must have been living righteously enough to deserve the blessing, for both Isaac and the Lord reaffirmed his right to the birthright.

7. The Lord has told us that Abraham, Isaac, and Jacob have already entered into their exaltation, "and sit upon thrones, and are not angels but are gods" (D&C 132:37).

Several men met with a General Authority in Salt Lake City for the purpose of being set apart as priesthood leaders. As the General Authority set apart the first man, he confused him with one of the other men and addressed him by the wrong name. As soon as the setting apart and blessing was finished, one of the men from the stake pointed out the mistake and suggested that the man would have to be set apart again. The General Authority quickly put this idea to rest by explaining that, even though he had thought the man was someone else, the Lord knew who the man was and had inspired him to give the right blessing to the right man.

The situation with Jacob and Esau is very similar. Even though Isaac thought he was blessing Esau, the Lord knew he was blessing Jacob and must have inspired him to give the right blessing to the right person. This may very well be why Isaac said the blessing would stand—he knew that the blessing he had given had come from the Lord.

Two valuable lessons can be learned from this story of Jacob and Esau. The first lesson is taught to us by Esau. After learning that Jacob had received the birthright blessing, Esau said, "Bless me, even me also, O my father," and then "lifted up his voice, and wept" (Genesis 27:38).

Sometimes, like Esau, we desire certain blessings from God but fail to live the laws that make these blessings possible. The scripture quoted above (D&C 130:20–21) emphasizes the importance of obedience in receiving blessings from God.

Blessings from the windows of heaven are poured out on those who pay tithing, and similarly, forgiveness is reserved for those who truly repent. Spiritual growth comes to those who pray, study, and strive to serve the Lord. Personal revelation is received when our hearts are pure and our minds are focused on the things of God. An eternal marriage takes more than just going to the temple to be sealed, and happiness does not spring automatically from Church membership. Everything of value has a price, and the precious blessings of heaven are no exception.

The second concept we can learn springs from Jacob and Rebekah's deception of Isaac. They were both great people, yet their faith in Isaac and in the Lord may not have been as strong as it could have been. They should have known that the Lord would not allow the wrong person to receive the birthright, and it appears that they underestimated God's power in directing his servants here upon the earth. Even though he was old and had indicated a course that seemed contrary to God's will, Isaac was still the Lord's anointed and surely would have received the proper inspiration before giving the blessing to Esau.

Some latter-day prophets have become old and feeble while in office, but God has never allowed them to lead the Church astray. Great blessings come to us and to the Church collectively when we sustain, support, and obey those who have been given leadership positions over us. This includes priesthood and Relief Society leaders, bishops and stake presidents, and all those who have been ordained or set apart through the authority of the holy priesthood of God. The Lord put it this way: "For he that receiveth my servants receiveth me; and he that receiveth me receiveth my Father; and he that receiveth my Father receiveth my Father's kingdom; therefore all that my Father hath shall be given unto him." (D&C 84:36–38.)

As we put the Lord first in our lives and decide to obey not only his written word but also the guidance of his living servants, we become eligible to receive all the blessings that our Heavenly Father desires to bestow upon us. These blessings include peace, guidance, and happiness in this life, and eternal life and a fulness of joy in the life to come.

15

Joseph and His Brothers

GENESIS 29–30, 37

Joseph, the son of Jacob, was one of the most righteous men who ever lived, yet the first thirty years of his life were filled with heartache and adversity. However, rather than blame God for the negative things that happened to him, Joseph remained faithful and received great spiritual and physical blessings.

As a teenager, Joseph faced much resentment and hate within his own family. Some of these bitter feelings probably came from the discord that existed among his father's wives. As you remember, after Jacob had worked seven years for the hand of Rachel, her father, Laban, deceived Jacob by switching Rachel for her older sister, Leah. Jacob did not discover until the morning after the wedding that he had married the wrong sister. When he confronted Laban, the father of the two girls, he was told that he would have to work another seven years for Rachel. Because of his great love for her, he was willing to do this.

This deception left Leah in a very awkward position—she wanted Jacob's love, but he loved Rachel deeply. Leah's desire to gain Jacob's acceptance and love is clearly seen in the names she gave her sons. As a matter of fact, most of the names of the twelve sons of Jacob illustrate the rivalry, real or imagined, that Leah and Rachel felt for Jacob's love.

When Leah's first son was born, she called him Reuben,

which means "Look, a son," and said, "Surely the Lord hath looked upon my affliction; now therefore my husband will love me" (Genesis 29:32).

She named her second son Simeon, which means "hearing," and exclaimed, "Because the Lord hath heard that I was hated, he hath therefore given me this son also." She called her third son Levi, which means "joined," and declared, "Now this time will my husband be joined unto me." (Genesis 29:33–34.)

As was often done in Old Testament times, both Leah and Rachel had received handmaids when they were married. Zilpah was the handmaid for Leah, and Bilhah was Rachel's handmaid. If a wife was barren, she could ask her husband to marry her handmaid; any children from this marriage would be counted as the original wife's children. A good example of this was Abraham and Sarah. After bearing no children for many years, Sarah told Abraham to take Hagar, her maid, as a wife so that she might be able to "obtain children by her." Abraham obeyed Sarah's wish, and Ishmael was born. (See Genesis 16.)

After Leah's fourth child was born, Rachel, who was barren, envying her sister, asked Jacob to take Bilhah, her handmaid, to wife "that I may also have children by her." Bilhah conceived and gave Jacob a son, whom Rachel named Dan. The name Dan means "God has judged, or vindicated," and Rachel said, "God hath judged me, . . . and hath given me a son." After Bilhah had another son, Rachel announced, "With great wrestlings have I wrestled with my sister, and I have prevailed: and she called his name Naphtali," which means "My wrestling." (See Genesis 30:1–8.)

Leah then gave her handmaid to Jacob, and the contest went on until twelve sons were born in all. Joseph was the first-born son of Rachel and the eleventh son born to Jacob.

Although some of the envy and strife that existed between Joseph and his older brothers probably was a product of their mothers, other events took place that intensified these feelings. One of these events revolved around the "coat of many colors." When Jacob gave Joseph the coat, his brothers "hated him, and could not speak peaceably unto him" (Genesis 37:4). This is because the coat represented much more than a nice gift or a beautiful piece of clothing; it was an obvious sign that Jacob favored Joseph above his brothers.

The LDS Bible footnote says that the Hebrew term may indicate "a long coat with sleeves." Another source states that "Joseph received a tunic of many pieces. The additional pieces were probably long sleeves that were a nuisance and got in the way when work was to be done. . . . This indicated that Joseph was not expected to do heavy work; he was the chosen heir to rule over the family." (Ralph Gower, *The New Manners and Customs of Bible Times* [Chicago: Moody Press, 1987], p. 20.)

This type of coat may still be in existence in the Old World. There are Bedouin tribes today that live very much as Abraham, Isaac, and Jacob did thousands of years ago. While visiting Israel, some Church members had an opportunity to visit one of these Bedouin tribes. The leader of the tribe wore a coat that had sleeves that touched the ground when he held his arms straight out in front of him. The sleeves were a normal size at the undercrarms, but many pieces of cloth had been stitched together to make the sleeves larger and larger until they were three or four feet wide at the wrists. The Bedouin leader said that this coat represented his authority to lead his people.

Regardless of what the coat looked like, Joseph's brothers saw it as a sign that Jacob intended to pass them by and make Joseph his heir. This makes a lot of sense, since Reuben, the firstborn, had sinned when he "lay with Bilhah his father's concubine" (Genesis 35:22); since Joseph was the firstborn son of the second wife, he was next in line to receive the birthright blessing. The idea of their younger brother ruling over them, however, did not appeal to Joseph's older brothers.

Joseph's dreams added additional fuel to their jealousy and hate. In one dream, the family was in a field binding sheaves. The sheaf that Joseph was binding arose and stood upright. The brothers' sheaves made obeisance to Joseph's sheaf. After hearing of this dream, the brothers "hated him yet the more for his dreams, and for his words." (See Genesis 37:5–8.)

In Joseph's second dream, the sun, the moon, and eleven stars made obeisance to him. The family knew what the dream meant, for Jacob declared, "Shall I and thy mother and thy brethren indeed come to bow down ourselves to thee to the earth?" His brothers were filled with envy, but his father "observed the saying." (Genesis 37:9–11.)

This was the temperament of Joseph's brothers when

Joseph was sent to see how they and the sheep were doing. When the brothers saw him coming "afar off," they discussed ways they could kill him. That Joseph's dreams had really rankled them is apparent, for they said to each other, "Behold, this dreamer cometh."

The suggestion was made that they slay Joseph, cast him into a pit, and tell their father that some wild beast had devoured him. One of the brothers then added, "And we shall see what will become of his dreams."

Reuben had reason to resent Joseph the most, for Joseph had replaced him as the birthright son, yet it was Reuben who tried to save his life. Reuben suggested that they not kill Joseph but just leave him in a pit to die. He was planning on returning to the pit after the brothers had left and safely delivering Joseph to their father.

The brothers decided to follow Reuben's plan, and, when Joseph arrived, they removed his birthright coat and cast him into an empty pit to die. Reuben separated himself from his brothers so that he would be able to return and help Joseph, and the rest of the brothers sat down to eat. Looking up and seeing an Ishmaelite caravan traveling toward Egypt, Judah said to his brothers, "What profit is it if we slay our brother, and conceal his blood." Judah suggested that if they sold him, they would become richer and his blood would not be upon their hands. The brothers quickly agreed with Judah's plan, and Joseph was soon headed for the slave markets of Egypt.

The brothers then killed a goat, dipped Joseph's coat in its blood, and later gave the coat to their father. Jacob, thinking that an animal had devoured Joseph, ripped his clothes, put on sackcloth, and mourned for his son.

The next sentence in the story carries a powerful message, a message that can be applied to many facets of our lives today. The scripture says that "all his sons and all his daughters rose up to comfort him; but he refused to be comforted." (See Genesis 37:15–35.)

What a farce this must have been—the brothers guiltily attempting to comfort their father, knowing that they were the cause of his mourning. His sons "rose up to comfort him" but failed to do those things that would bring true comfort. They failed to tell Jacob that his son was still alive and made no attempt to follow the caravan and possibly bring Joseph back. Jacob's sons gave empty words in the place of healing actions.

This same problem exists in the homes of many families today. Some parents say they would do anything to have a better relationship with their children, yet they fail to give the time, interest, and patience that would bring this relationship about. Many children profess love for their parents and give them gifts on holidays and birthdays but fail to give the one gift the parents desire most—the gift of righteousness and obedience.

A bishop was approached by a couple who desired help with their marriage. They indicated that they would do anything to make their marriage work. When the bishop suggested that they start coming to church and that they begin to apply gospel principles in their home, they said they could not see what gospel teachings had to do with their marriage problems and left in a huff.

So many times, family members give things instead of time and offer words instead of actions. Like Jacob's sons, they go through the motions of love and concern but don't give of themselves. On the other hand, numerous children and adults do give their loved ones gifts of comfort, peace, and happiness. This type of giving was exemplified by a young son who, instead of giving his father a necktie or a handkerchief for Father's Day, gave a glimpse into his heart and the will to live the gospel. This loving son slipped the following letter under his Dad's pillow on Father's Day.

Dad:

I love you for what you are and not for what you aren't. Why don't you stop smoking? Millions of people have . . . why can't you? It's harmful to your health, to your lungs, your heart. If you can't keep the Word of Wisdom you can't go to heaven with me, Skip, Brad, Marc, Jeff, Jeannie, Pam, and their families. Us kids keep the Word of Wisdom. Why can't you? You are stronger and you are a man. Dad, I want to see you in heaven. We all do. We want to be a whole family in heaven . . . not half of one.

Dad, you and Mom ought to get two old bikes and start riding around the park every night. You are probably laughing right now, but I wouldn't be. You laugh at those old people, jogging around the park and riding bikes and walking, but they are going to outlive you. Because they are exercising their lungs, their hearts, their muscles. They are going to have the last laugh.

Come on, Dad, be a good guy—don't smoke, drink, or anything else against our religion. We want you at our graduation. If you do quit smoking and do good stuff like us, you and Mom can go with Brother Monson and get married and sealed to us in the temple.

Come on, Dad—Mom and us kids are just waiting for you. We want to live with you forever. We love you. You're the greatest, Dad.

Love,

Todd

P.S. And if the rest of us wrote one of these, they'd say the same thing.

P.P.S. Mr. Newton has quit smoking. So can you. You are closer to God than Mr. Newton! (Thomas S. Monson, "The Prayer of Faith," *Ensign*, May 1978, pp. 21–22.)

After receiving this precious gift from his son, the father soon assembled with his family in a sacred room in the temple to be sealed as an eternal family. This young boy gave that which was truly needed, and the blessings from this gift will extend throughout eternity. All of us have the power to bless the lives of our loved ones with gifts of true value. As we strive to give those things that our families really need, the Lord will direct our thoughts and our actions. Then, unlike the sons of Jacob, we will bring increased peace, comfort, and joy to those we love the most.

16

The Lord Was with Joseph

GENESIS 39

The story of Joseph in Egypt is one of strength, courage, and total commitment to God. As a slave, as a prisoner, and as a ruler of Egypt, his standards remained the same. Neither adversity, betrayal, riches, nor power affected his devotion and faithfulness.

Joseph was sold as a slave to an Egyptian named Potiphar, the captain of Pharaoh's guard. Because of Joseph's unwavering faith and dedication, the Lord blessed him. Potiphar was a rich man, and he soon noticed that "the Lord was with [Joseph], and that the Lord made all that he did to prosper in his hand." Joseph found "grace in [Potiphar's] sight" and was soon placed over all that Potiphar owned.

From the moment that Joseph became responsible for Potiphar's property, the "Lord blessed the Egyptian's house for Joseph's sake." Potiphar trusted Joseph completely, and Joseph handled the record keeping as well as the administration of his property. (See Genesis 39:1–6.)

The scriptures state that Joseph was well favored, implying that he was physically attractive, and that he had been blessed with many talents. Potiphar's wife became attracted to Joseph, and she asked him to lie with her. He referred to the great trust that Potiphar had placed in him and explained that he could not betray this trust. Joseph then revealed his great commitment to God when he said, "How then can I do this great wickedness, and sin against God?" (Genesis 39:9.)

Joseph's rejection of Potiphar's wife only seemed to fuel her desire for him, for "day by day" she pressed him to "lie by her, or to be with her." She was likely applying a great deal of pressure to get Joseph to succumb to her desires. One day, when Joseph was alone in the house with her, she "caught him by his garment, saying, Lie with me: and he left his garment in her hand, and fled, and got him out." (Genesis 39:11–12.)

What a great message for us all! When Joseph found himself in a spiritually dangerous situation, he removed himself immediately. He was more concerned about moral cleanliness and avoiding temptation than finding a pleasant way to say no. The spiritual consequences of sin were more important to him than the physical repercussions of making an enemy of his master's wife. He valued chastity and obedience even more than life itself.

The findings of several studies concerning teenagers indicate that, far and away, the number one reason for teenagers doing things they know are wrong is to gain or keep the acceptance of their peers. In contrast, Joseph was more concerned about earning God's acceptance.

Joseph had the strength and confidence to stand up for the right because he realized who he was—a precious and literal son of God. This divine sense of self-worth was a product of his righteousness and came through revelation from the Lord. Stephen R. Covey said, "To live a life that is congruent and harmonious with Jesus Christ, our Savior and Redeemer, is the highest source of intrinsic security." Brother Covey further taught that when we are true to the light we have been given, we receive "a sense of peace and unity and wholeness—a sense of internal worth." (*Spiritual Roots of Human Relations* [Salt Lake City: Deseret Book Co., 1970], p. 89.) God has declared that those who are virtuous and charitable will receive great confidence, even to the extent that they will feel confident in His presence (see D&C 121:45). Joseph's confidence to stand up against his master's wife came from his years of faithfulness and obedience.

Evidently Potiphar's wife felt that she had been snubbed for the last time: she called in the servants, showed them Joseph's garment, and told them that Joseph had tried to force her to lie with him. When her husband arrived home, she told him the same story. The fact that he put Joseph in prison instead of having him killed may suggest that he really didn't believe Joseph was guilty but had to do something in order to keep peace with his wife. A servant forcing himself upon the master's wife in that society would usually lead to certain death.

Even with this setback, Joseph stayed faithful and the Lord "shewed him mercy, and gave him favour in the sight of the keeper of the prison. And the keeper of the prison committed to Joseph's hand all the prisoners that were in the prison." Total control over the prison was given to Joseph "because the Lord was with him, and that which he did, the Lord made it to prosper." (Genesis 39:21–23.)

The interesting thing about Joseph is that he was more free in prison than his brothers were at home. There are four realms of freedom, and, in order to be truly free, we need to be free in all four of these areas. The four areas of freedom are physical, emotional, spiritual, and mental. Joseph's brothers were free physically, but they were not free in the other three areas. They lived in spiritual bondage; suffered spiritual, mental, and emotional guilt; and knew they were not right with either their earthly father or their Heavenly Father.

Joseph, on the other hand, was in physical bondage but was free in the other three areas of his life. He was free from a guilty conscience; free to receive help, inspiration, and comfort from God; and felt comfortable with both himself and with the Lord.

In order to be truly free, we need to make correct choices. Jesus emphasized this when he said, "If ye continue in my word, then are ye my disciples indeed; and ye shall know the truth, and the truth shall make you free." (John 8:31–32.)

The more correct choices we make, the more choices we have available to us. Incorrect choices lead to fewer choices and less freedom. Keeping or breaking the Word of Wisdom is an easy example to follow and illustrates this principle well.

If we decide to smoke, we restrict our freedom of choice in so many ways. Physically, we restrict our performance in almost any activity we participate in. Studies indicate that a majority of adults who smoke want to quit but feel they cannot. They have lost the freedom to decide whether they will smoke.

Disobedience, however, nearly always affects us spiritually more than in any other way, and the Word of Wisdom is no exception. When we decide to disobey the Word of Wisdom and do so permanently, we lose the opportunity to receive the full promptings of the Holy Ghost. We cannot participate in the ordinances of the temple. Advancement in the priesthood is ruled out, and we limit the callings in the Church that are available to us. We even significantly limit our opportunity and ability to counsel our children wisely and encourage them to live the gospel. Most of all, we limit the choices we will have for all eternity by making a choice that will prevent us from attaining exaltation in the celestial kingdom.

When we live the Word of Wisdom, we open up all of these other choices and still do not limit our freedom in any way. We can still smoke if we want to—we have simply decided that we don't want to. At times we hear people complain about how restrictive the Church is. Actually, it is exactly the opposite. Through helping its members understand the gospel and make correct choices, the Church helps us become more free than any other people on the face of the earth.

Allowing ourselves to be controlled by circumstances instead of taking control of our own lives and feelings is another factor that can limit our freedom. God has given us the power to overcome our circumstances. Lehi said that because of the atonement of Christ we are free "to act for ourselves and not . . . be acted upon." Lehi went on to say that all things have been given to us that we need so that we are "free to choose liberty and eternal life, through the great Mediator of all men, or to choose captivity and death, according to the captivity and power of the devil." (2 Nephi 2:26–27.)

Although we are free to act for ourselves, we sometimes allow people or circumstances to decide how we will feel and what we will say or do. If we meet someone who is angry, we become angry. If someone yells at us, we yell back. We allow others to be the control center for our feelings, and even our actions, by reacting to them instead of acting for ourselves.

It appears that sometime in his youth Joseph developed the desire and strength to control his actions, and hence enjoyed more peace and happiness than those who physically ruled over him. Blanche Scow is a perfect latter-day example of someone who is restricted physically yet is more free than many around her.

Blanche was in her early thirties when she entered the hospital for minor surgery. She left the hospital paralyzed because of a mistake made during the operation. When her alcoholic husband learned of her incapacity, he left her and their four children to fend for themselves. At first she was upset, but she soon realized that her children needed her and she went about the business of raising them.

Blanche harbored no bitterness for her husband, her doctor, or her circumstances. For over thirty years she was confined to a wheelchair. Then, because of a stroke, she became totally bedridden. Still her attitude toward life was upbeat and positive. Talking about her total confinement to her bed, she said, "I must be here for a purpose. . . . Now that I can't get into my wheelchair, I have to just keep plugging along. But I have so much to be grateful for. I count my blessings every day. For instance, last weekend my granddaughter came by with her husband and baby. Little children are precious, and they grow up so fast. I have a lot to live for. . . . I am so grateful I can see."

A young mother who was confined to her bed during a difficult pregnancy would call Blanche on especially difficult days and receive the strength and encouragement that she needed. This mother later wrote, "As the weeks went by, I knew that I would soon be released from my confinement. Blanche knew that she would remain. But she taught me that nothing can really confine a person's heart and soul. I knew that, in many ways, she was a much freer person than I." (Janene Wolsey Baadsgaard, "The Unconfined Heart," *Ensign,* April 1988, pp. 47–48.)

Through the examples of both Blanche and Joseph, we learn that we can react to life in a positive way and, with the help of the Lord, overcome any adversity we are faced with. Their lives teach us that freedom has more to do with attitude and righteousness than events and circumstances and that the Lord will always be close to us if we will strive to stay close to him.

17

Joseph Becomes a Ruler

GENESIS 40–41

Members of the Church living in Tonga have a difficult time taking advantage of the covenants and blessings available in the temple. The closest temple to Tonga is in New Zealand, and most Tongan families cannot afford to make the long and expensive journey.

One family in Tonga received strong spiritual promptings that they should travel to New Zealand and obtain their temple blessings. In order to do so, they would need to sell all that they owned, including their modest hut. They made the decision that obedience to the Holy Ghost and receiving the blessings of the temple were more important than any earthly possessions, so they proceeded to sell all of their furniture and personal belongings. They found that they could get more for their hut if they dismantled it and sold each piece separately, so this is what they did. Their friends in the Church made fun of them and tried to talk them out of their "foolishness." The family was told over and over again that God did not expect them to sacrifice everything they had in order to go to the temple. They responded that they could not speak for others, but they knew that this is what God wanted their family to do.

This devoted family traveled to New Zealand and eagerly partook of the spirit and blessings of the temple. Just two

weeks after they returned home, a hurricane swept through
their area and destroyed everything in its path. Everyone
around them lost their homes and all of their belongings. The
family quickly realized the temple trip had actually cost them
nothing, for they would have lost everything anyway. Because
they had been responsive to the whisperings of the Spirit, even
though they possessed no physical riches, they enjoyed the precious promises and blessings of a covenant family.

The Savior counseled, "Lay not up for yourselves treasures
upon earth, where moth and rust doth corrupt, . . . but lay up
for yourselves treasures in heaven, where neither moth nor rust
doth corrupt." (Matthew 6:19–20.) All those in the area had
lost all of their earthly riches in a matter of hours, but this
family still possessed the heavenly riches of the temple in abun-
dance. Only personal unrighteousness could ever take these
blessings away from them.

Probably we will never know whether at that time God
prompted other families in the area to go to the temple, but we
do know this: God's knowledge and vision are infinitely greater
than ours, and he desires to share his knowledge with us. This
family benefited greatly by responding to the guidance and will
of God.

God has plans for us that far exceed our present goals and
expectations, for we possess talents and abilities that we know
nothing of. God not only knows us better than we know ourselves but is also aware of future conditions and situations that
can benefit both us and his kingdom if we are responsive to his
will. Such was the case with Joseph in Egypt. It is highly
unlikely that he ever envisioned himself becoming an important
leader of Egypt and being in a position to save his family from
starvation and death, yet the Lord was moving him toward this
end throughout his life.

One reason for Joseph's dreams as a young man may have
been to help him understand the process of revelation through
dreams, for this was the means God used to elevate him from a
lowly prisoner to the chief ruler over all of Egypt. Sometime
after Joseph had been placed in charge over the other prisoners, the Pharaoh's chief butler and baker offended Pharaoh so
he had them thrown into prison. They were both placed under
Joseph's direction. Both of these men had dreams that caused

them to feel uncomfortable. Joseph explained to them that the interpretation of dreams belonged to God and then proceeded, with the help of God, to interpret the butler's dream. He told the chief butler that in three days he would be returned to his place in Pharaoh's service; and he said, "Think on me when it shall be well with thee, and shew kindness, I pray thee, unto me, and make mention of me unto Pharaoh, and bring me out of this house" (Genesis 40:14).

When the chief baker saw that the butler's dream had a happy ending, he asked Joseph to interpret his dream. This turned out to be a mistake, for he was told that in three days the Pharaoh would have him executed.

Both these interpretations came to pass, just as Joseph had explained them, yet the chief butler forgot all about Joseph and failed to mention him to the Pharaoh.

Two full years later, Pharaoh dreamed of seven fat cows that came out of the river and fed in a meadow. He then saw seven lean cows come out of the river and devour the seven fat cows. This dream was followed by another in which seven thin ears of corn devoured seven good ears.

Pharaoh's spirit was troubled. When he asked his magicians and wise men to interpret his dreams, none of them could do it. It is incredible that none of the wise men could interpret these dreams, for they were well versed in Egyptian symbolism, and the dreams contained common symbols of their day. For example, the cow was the symbol of Isis, the goddess of the all-sustaining earth; therefore, the cow represented the food that came from the earth. It appears that, just as God inspired Joseph to interpret the dreams, he caused a stupor of thought to come upon the magicians and the wise men.

When none of the wise men could tell the king what the dreams meant, the chief butler finally remembered Joseph and his power to interpret dreams. Pharaoh sent for Joseph immediately, but Joseph would not come until he had shaved himself and changed his clothing. He knew that often appearance can influence the lives of others. Because of this influence, missionaries today still shave themselves and put on their best clothing before leaving their apartments as representatives of the Lord.

When Pharaoh asked Joseph if he could interpret dreams, he told him it was God, not Joseph, who did the interpreting.

After Pharaoh had related his dreams, Joseph told him that the dreams had come from God; and that there would be seven years of plenty followed by seven years of famine. Joseph suggested that Pharaoh choose a wise man and set him over the land of Egypt to direct the gathering of a fifth part of the harvest during the seven plenteous years. Pharaoh then said, "Can we find such a one as this is, a man in whom the Spirit of God is?" (Genesis 41:38) and he placed Joseph next to him in power and authority. Pharaoh's ring was placed on Joseph's finger and he was dressed in fine linen with a gold chain around his neck.

Joseph became a ruler over Egypt when he was thirty years old, which means that he served as a slave and then a prisoner for perhaps a dozen long years. Most of the time Joseph was probably praying simply for freedom, but God had a much greater work in mind. God sees our potential and needs much differently than we do, as illustrated by an experience that happened in the life of Wendy Rudder.

Wendy lived on a ranch in Wyoming with her husband and children. Their winter had been a cold one; by January the snow was piled up to the eaves of the porch. The pasture was covered under many feet of snow, and the horses received their food and water only by snowmobile. One January evening, the phone rang: Wendy was told that their horses had wandered out onto the railroad tracks. Her husband was not home, so it became her job to get on the snowmobile and herd the horses back to safety. After searching for a while without any success, Wendy decided to cross the tracks and see if the horses had returned to the pasture where they belonged.

It was too dark for Wendy to see that the snow had melted from the tracks. When she went to cross them, the snowmobile came to a sudden halt with the front of the skis tightly wedged underneath the track. While pulling at the snowmobile with all of her might, she prayed, "Help me, Heavenly Father, help me!"

And Heavenly Father did help her, but not in the way that she expected. A thought came to her mind: "If a train comes around that corner you'll never hear it until it's too late. Get that helmet off your head!"

After she removed the helmet, the light of a freight train appeared around the bend and she heard a voice say, "You have three children at home. *Get off the tracks!*"

Wendy left the snowmobile to its own fate and ran from the tracks as quickly as she could. She turned around just in time to see the train hit the snowmobile and throw it 150 yards down the track. As she realized what could have happened to her, she began to shake and walked most of the way home in a condition of shock.

The next morning, she went with her family to find the snowmobile. "Pieces were strewn everywhere. Only a twisted part of the body of the sled remained intact." That evening, her four-year-old boy said in his bedtime prayer, "Thanks for keeping Mommy safe."

Wendy summed up this experience by saying: "I know our Heavenly Father answers prayers. I also know that our prayers are not always answered in the way we expect. But in my case, I was given what I really needed. My prayer for help did not allow me to save the snow machine, but it did save my life." (Wendy R. Rudder, "Get Off the Tracks!" *Ensign*, January 1988, pp. 50–51.)

Joseph was praying for freedom, and God made him a governor. Wendy was praying for help in saving her snowmobile, and God saved her life instead. Sometimes, when we find ourselves suffering through what we consider serious problems or overwhelming adversity, all we seek is relief from our problems. God seeks to give us the experiences necessary to become kings and queens, priests and priestesses. If we will trust in his expanded vision and infinite wisdom, he will bestow upon us blessings that we have never even considered before: "Eye hath not seen, nor ear heard, neither have entered into the heart of man, the things which God hath prepared for them that love him" (1 Corinthians 2:9).

18

Joseph Saves His Family

GENESIS 42–46

Because of God's foresight and planning, Egypt escaped the famine that spread across the face of the land. As people from surrounding countries poured into Egypt to buy grain, they were sent to Joseph. When Jacob's family ran out of food in the land of Canaan, Joseph's ten older brothers were sent to obtain grain in Egypt. Jacob kept Joseph's younger brother, Benjamin, at home, lest he should come to harm.

As the brothers were ushered into Joseph's presence they "bowed down . . . before him with their faces to the earth." Even though they did not recognize him, Joseph recognized them immediately and "made himself strange unto them, and spake roughly unto them" so that they would not realize who he was. (Genesis 42:6–7.) They may not have recognized Joseph for several reasons. It had been more than twenty years since they had sold him into slavery, and he had grown from a boy to a mature man. Even if he looked somewhat like the Joseph they remembered, they would never have thought that the governor of Egypt was their younger brother.

Joseph still loved his brothers, and, as will be discussed later, he had forgiven them completely. He might have wondered whether his brothers had changed any since they had sold him as a slave, for he set up a plan that would bring out their true character and feelings. Joseph accused them of being spies. When they claimed they were brothers and had left a younger brother at home, Joseph established a way for them to prove their innocence. He explained to them that one of them would be sent to bring back the younger brother while the rest would be held in prison. He then locked them up for three days while they made their decision.

Joseph's plan was a great one, for it truly would reveal whether they had changed over the past twenty years. Benjamin's situation in the family was very similar to Joseph's when the brothers had resented and hated him. If they hated and resented Benjamin, they probably had not changed. But if they showed love and concern for Benjamin and for the feelings of their father, it would demonstrate that they had matured spiritually and emotionally.

At the end of the three days, Joseph told his brothers, "This do, and live. . . . If ye be true men, let one of your brethren be bound in the house of your prison: go ye, carry corn for the famine of your houses: but bring your youngest brother unto me; so shall your words be verified, and ye shall not die." (Genesis 42:18–20.)

What happened next gives us a wonderful insight into the hearts of the brothers. Knowing of the great love their father had for Benjamin and how much it would hurt their father to lose him, their true feelings concerning Joseph came to the surface. It is apparent that for twenty-two years they had lived with guilt and pain, for they said to each other, "We are verily guilty concerning our brother, in that we saw the anguish of his soul, when he besought us, and we would not hear; therefore is this distress come upon us" (Genesis 42:21). Reuben even reminded them that he had told them not to sin against Joseph, and he reiterated their fears that Benjamin was now placed in danger because of their actions against Joseph.

Because Joseph spoke through an interpreter, they did not realize that he could understand them. When Joseph saw how guilty they felt about their treatment of him and realized how much they loved Benjamin, he turned away from them and wept. It must have been very difficult for Joseph to continue to conceal who he was, but he gained control of his emotions and proceeded with his plan.

Joseph took Simeon away from them and had him bound in front of their eyes. He commanded his servants to fill their sacks with grain and to secretly replace their money in each sack. They were then sent on their way. When the money was discovered, the hearts of both them and Jacob were filled with fear. After hearing what had taken place in Egypt, Jacob lamented, "Joseph is not, and Simeon is not, and ye will take Benjamin away: all these things are against me" (Genesis 42:36).

The great love that Reuben had for his father surfaced, and he said, "Slay my two sons, if I bring him not to thee: deliver him into my hand, and I will bring him to thee again" (Genesis 42:37).

In spite of Reuben's assurance that he would protect Benjamin, Jacob would not allow them to return with Benjamin to Egypt. This decision was temporary, however, for they soon ran short of food again. Jacob was still hesitant about letting Benjamin go, so Judah stepped forward and said, "I will be surety for him; of my hand shalt thou require him: if I bring him not unto thee, and set him before thee, then let me bear the blame for ever" (Genesis 43:9).

The brothers armed themselves with presents, double the amount of money they took the first time, and their younger brother, and apprehensively set off for Egypt.

When they arrived, the brothers were brought to Joseph's house. Joseph asked them about the health of their father, and, when his eyes rested upon Benjamin, his own mother's son, "Joseph made haste; for his bowels did yearn upon his brother: and he sought where to weep; and he entered into his chamber, and wept there" (Genesis 43:30). He then washed his face and joined his brothers in a meal.

Joseph then set the final and most important phase of his test into operation. After filling their sacks with grain, he had his personal silver cup placed in Benjamin's sack. Shortly after the brothers had left for home, Joseph sent his servant after them. When Joseph's servant caught up with them, he accused them of stealing Joseph's silver cup.

The brothers claimed they were innocent and even said that if the cup were found in one of their sacks, the owner of the sack should be killed and the rest of the brothers would become servants to the governor. Joseph's servant said, "Let it be according unto your words," and they began to search the sacks. They started with the oldest brother's sack and worked down until Benjamin's sack was the last one searched. When the cup was found in his sack, the brothers "rent their clothes" in despair. Quickly they returned to the city.

Once again the guilt the brothers felt concerning their treatment of Joseph surfaced, for Judah exclaimed, "What shall we say unto my lord? what shall we speak? or how shall we clear ourselves? God hath found out the iniquity of thy servants." (Genesis 44:16.) Judah then offered himself and his brothers as servants to Joseph.

When Joseph declared that Benjamin would be his servant and the rest of the brothers were free to go, Judah opened his heart to Joseph and pleaded in Benjamin's behalf. His pleas allowed Joseph to discern that Judah and his brothers were truly repentant and that they felt a great love for both Benjamin and their father. Judah said to Joseph, "We have a father, an old man, and a child of his old age, a little one; and his brother is dead, and he alone is left of his mother, and his father loveth him" (Genesis 44:20).

Judah seemed to be able to talk about Jacob's special love for Benjamin without the jealousy and bitterness that he had earlier felt towards Joseph. He explained that Benjamin was the son of his father's old age and that if they returned without him, it would kill his father. Judah then volunteered himself in the place of Benjamin by saying: "I pray thee, let thy servant abide instead of the lad a bondman to my lord; and let the lad go up with his brethren. For how shall I go up to my father, and the lad be not with me? lest peradventure I see the evil that shall come on my father." (Genesis 44:33–34.)

Joseph, finding that he could restrain himself no longer, asked his servants to leave the room and told his brothers who he was. This confused and troubled his brothers a great deal, so he asked them to come near him and declared:

I am Joseph your brother, whom ye sold into Egypt.

Now therefore be not grieved, nor angry with yourselves, that ye sold me hither: for God did send me before you to preserve life. . . .

So now it was not you that sent me hither, but God: and
he hath made me a father to Pharaoh, and lord of all his
house, and a ruler throughout all the land of Egypt.

Haste ye, and go up to my father, and say unto him, Thus
saith thy son Joseph, God hath made me lord of all Egypt:
come down unto me, tarry not. (Genesis 45:4–5, 8–9.)

Joseph then fell upon Benjamin's neck and wept, and "Benjamin wept upon his neck." He then kissed each one of his
brothers and "wept upon them." His brothers then returned
quickly to the land of Canaan and told their father the good
news. When Jacob saw the wagons that Joseph had sent to
carry him, his spirit was revived and he said, "It is enough;
Joseph my son is yet alive: I will go and see him before I die"
(Genesis 45:28).

While they were on their way to Egypt, the Lord spoke to
Jacob and said: "Fear not to go down into Egypt; for I will there
make of thee a great nation: I will go down with thee into
Egypt; and I will also surely bring thee up again." (Genesis
45:3–4.) God surely did make of Jacob a great nation, for only
seventy souls entered Egypt at the time of Joseph, and millions
of Israelites left four hundred years later under Moses' direction.

One of the great lessons to be learned from this story is that
people truly can change. Too often we judge people by what
they have done in the past, but Joseph accepted his brothers
for what they had become. Judah is a great example of spiritual
growth, for it was he that suggested they sell Joseph into Egypt.
Yet, twenty years later, he was willing to substitute himself for
Benjamin and become a slave for the rest of his life so that
Benjamin could be reunited with his father.

The gospel of Jesus Christ contains the power to change the
hearts and souls of men and women. Sometimes this change
happens quickly, but most of the time it takes place gradually.
The important thing is that it happens to everyone who opens
his heart to the Spirit and to the word of God.

Another critical truth this story teaches is the importance of
forgiving those who offend us. Joseph never would have had the
Spirit of the Lord to help him during his years of captivity if he
had been carrying feelings of bitterness and revenge in his soul.

Because he was able to purge his heart of these destructive forces, he received great blessings from the Lord. Much of the heartache and contention that exists in today's world stems from unforgiving hearts. Many times we are so busy condemning a person who has supposedly wronged us that we fail to realize we are committing a greater sin. Such was the case with Joaquim.

Joaquim had been a golden contact. After he and his family were baptized, they became pillars of strength in his branch. He was called to teach a Sunday School class, which he did with great enthusiasm and zeal. Then one day the Sunday School president shortened the class time in order to solve a scheduling problem. When Joaquim objected, he felt he received an inconsiderate reply. A short time later, when the offending Sunday School president became the branch president, Joaquim quit coming to church, and no amount of reasoning from members or missionaries could get him to change his mind.

Two of the missionaries in the area decided to visit Joaquim one more time to see if they could persuade him to come back to church. After the usual argument, which got them nowhere, one of the missionaries was impressed to say, "But Brother Joaquim, have you forgiven him?"

This question seemed to strike Joaquim with great force. Since he had been the one who was offended, he had been waiting for the branch president to apologize to him. After thinking about this question, "he turned to his wife and asked if she thought it was possible that he had not forgiven his fellowman, as the Savior had commanded. She answered in the affirmative, and the situation was resolved." They returned to church the following Sunday. (Keith Nielson, "Joaquim Stopped Coming to Church," *Ensign,* February 1989, p. 62.)

Great blessings come to us as we accept that those around us are going to make mistakes and that we must forgive them of actions that have offended us. We always hurt ourselves more than others when we fail to forgive. Since most of us find it necessary to seek daily forgiveness from the Father, it only seems reasonable that we would be willing to forgive those who offend us. As we do this, the Spirit of the Lord can be with us, and, as with Joseph, we will receive strength and guidance from God.

19

The Israelites Become Slaves

EXODUS 1

From the time of Eve, women have played a vital role in the growth and success of the kingdom of God. Both the Old and New Testaments are filled with stories depicting their unwavering faith, selfless love, and unyielding courage. Mary of Magdala was the first to see the resurrected Jesus. A widow with her two mites taught us what it means to place God first in our lives. The qualities of love and loyalty were demonstrated by Ruth and Naomi. A starving widow and her son gave the last of their meal to Elijah and never hungered again. Esther placed her life on the line in order to save her people.

Many other heroic women have remained nameless yet contributed greatly to their families, to their people, and to God. Some of these heroines lived in Egypt during the time of Moses.

God had promised both Abraham and Jacob that the Israelite people would become numerous; he also chose Egypt as the place where this promise would be fulfilled. After Joseph and his brothers had passed away, "the children of Israel were fruitful, and increased abundantly, and multiplied, and waxed exceeding mighty; and the land was filled with them" (Exodus 1:7).

Eventually a new king came into power in Egypt who did

not know Joseph and felt no compassion or respect for the Israelite people. In fact, because the Israelites had increased until they outnumbered the Egyptians, he feared for the safety of his kingdom. In order to slow down the Israelites' growth and better control them, he placed them under bondage and appointed taskmasters to afflict them with bitter and rigorous burdens, "but the more they afflicted them, the more they multiplied and grew" (Exodus 1:12).

In frustration, the king gave special instructions to the women who served as midwives to the Hebrews. He commanded them to kill any male child that was born to an Israelite woman. "But the midwives feared God, and did not as the king of Egypt commanded them, but saved the men children alive" (Exodus 1:17). Even though this put their own lives in jeopardy, their faith in God was stronger than their fear of the king.

When the king asked the midwives why they were not following his instructions, they told him that the Hebrew women were more "lively" than the Egyptian women and that they delivered their children before the midwives could get to them. Because of the great courage and faith of the midwives, God dealt well with them and blessed them with children of their own.

That special love and courage that many women possess was exemplified by Mrs. Handy, a mother during the American Revolution. The British, under the direction of a Captain Haughton, had offered a bounty to a group of Indians for each American male they captured. They were promised eight dollars for each man, less for boys, and even less for scalps. In the early morning hours, the Indians quietly attacked a settlement. They moved from cabin to cabin, capturing the men they could and killing all those who resisted. As Mrs. Handy, with her seven-year-old son and her baby daughter, attempted to escape, several Indians caught her and took her boy away from her. She was told that they were going to take her son to Canada and make a warrior of him. She also found out that if he was too weak to make the journey, he would be killed along the way.

Instead of taking her baby girl and moving downstream to safety, Mrs. Handy decided that she would not leave without her son, and she sought out the British leader of the Indians.

After managing to cross the river, while carrying her baby daughter, she was told by Captain Haughton that he could not control the Indians—and really didn't want to.

When her son was brought into camp, she grabbed his hand. Even when she was threatened with knives and tomahawks, she refused to let go. In spite of their threats, she told the Indians that she would not leave her son and would follow them every step of the way to Canada if necessary. Soon eight other young boys were brought into camp, and she interceded in their behalf just as vigorously as she had for her own son. Finally, in exasperation, the Indians gave in to her demands— they left her and the children behind when they left for Canada. Carrying her baby and two of the boys, with the rest of the children clinging to her skirts, she recrossed the river and returned the children to safety. (See Boyd K. Packer, *Mothers* [Salt Lake City: Deseret Book Co., 1977, pp. 10–16.)

A major contribution made by women usually happens within the walls of their own homes. Discussing the importance of women in God's eternal plan, Elder Neal A. Maxwell said:

> The charity of good women is such that their "love makes no parade"; they are not glad "when others go wrong"; they are too busy serving to sit statusfully about, waiting to be offended. . . . God trusts women so much that He lets them bear and care for His spirit children. . . .
>
> When the real history of mankind is fully disclosed, will it feature the echoes of gunfire or the shaping sound of lullabies? The great armistices made by military men or the peacemaking of women in homes and in neighborhoods? Will what happened in cradles and kitchens prove to be more controlling than what happened in congresses? When the surf of the centuries has made the great pyramids so much sand, the everlasting family will still be standing, because it is a celestial institution, formed outside the telestial time. The women of God know this. ("The Women of God," *Ensign*, May 1978, pp. 10–11.)

Most women today face different challenges than the mothers and midwives did at the time of Moses. Moral, emotional, and intellectual dangers are more abundant than physical perils.

Today's women are besieged with the destructive doctrines of abortion, limiting family size for selfish reasons, and placing personal careers ahead of family responsibilities. Paying tribute to the millions of women who have resisted these doctrines, Elder Maxwell said, "We salute you, sisters, for the joy that is yours as you rejoice in a baby's first smile and as you listen with eager ear to a child's first day at school which bespeaks a special selflessness. . . . You rock a sobbing child without wondering if today's world is passing you by, because you know you hold tomorrow tightly in your arms." ("The Women of God," p. 10.)

Talking about those women whose desires for marriage and motherhood have not been met, Elder Maxwell added: "They make wise career choices even though they cannot now have the most choice career. Though in their second estate they do not have their first desire, they still overcome the world. These sisters who cannot now enrich the institution of their own marriage so often enrich other institutions in society. They do not withhold their blessings simply because some blessings are now withheld from them." ("The Women of God," p. 11.)

Our family recently met with another one and held home evening together. As part of the lesson, we played a game in which teams were to come up with things that would be useless without something else. For example, a toaster would be useless without electricity, and a hose would be useless without water. Some of the answers revealed how important women are in the eyes of others. For instance, one husband said that he would be useless without his wife, and a child indicated that a bishop would be useless without a Relief Society president. At first, I chuckled at this child's response, but as I thought of the time I had served as a bishop, I realized how much the Relief Society presidents in my ward had added to my effectiveness as a leader. Their compassion, understanding, and dedicated service gave me valuable insights and inspiration.

Just as God's covenant promises at the time of Moses were brought to pass through the faith and courage of the mothers and midwives, women are central figures in bringing to pass the fulfillment of God's promises in our day. Those who truly understand the gospel realize the great contribution women make throughout the world as they share great strength and encouragement through their selfless service and unconditional love.

20

The Lord Prepares Moses to Free Israelites

EXODUS 2

One of the great truths that reveals itself throughout the scriptures is that God is in control. Even though Satan's forces appear to seriously obstruct or even destroy God's great plan of happiness, because of God's infinite power and knowledge his plan continues to unfold and follow its prearranged course. Satan was sure that by getting Adam and Eve to partake of the fruit, he would be able to frustrate God's plan; instead, it only furthered the plan. Saul (later known as Paul) persecuted the Saints to such a degree that great havoc took place in the Church and the members were scattered throughout many parts of Judea and Samaria. But what seemed like a problem actually became a blessing as these members shared the gospel: the good news of the Atonement quickly spread to such other areas.

Moses' birth and youth exemplify well how persecution and hardship often lead to the attainment of God's plans and purposes. Moses was born with a death sentence on his head, as the king of Egypt had ordered all male Hebrew children killed immediately following birth. There is no way to comprehend the depth of anxiety and fear that Moses' mother must have felt as she hid him from the soldiers and spies for three long months. When she could no longer hide him, she built a small boat out of the bulrushes, daubed it with a waterproof substance, placed her baby in it, and floated it among the reeds that grew along the river's edge. She then sent Miriam, Moses' sister, to watch over the little boat and see what eventually happened to her three-month-old baby.

About this time, the daughter of Pharaoh came to the river to wash herself. When she saw the boat among the reeds, she sent one of her servants to fetch it for her. Moses was an exceeding fair baby (see Acts 7:20), so when the Pharaoh's daughter opened the ark and Moses wept, it is not surprising that her heart was filled with compassion.

When the Pharaoh's daughter recognized Moses as a Hebrew baby, Miriam stepped forward and volunteered to call a Hebrew woman to nurse the child for her. Of course, Miriam returned with her mother, who received wages from Pharaoh's daughter for nursing and teaching her own child. It is very easy to identify the hand of the Lord throughout this inspiring story.

Pharaoh's daughter raised Moses as her own son, which meant that he was educated in all the wisdom of the Egyptians. Moses became mighty in word and deed and received great power as a prince in Egypt. (See Acts 7:21–22.)

The Jewish historian Josephus recorded amazing accounts of Moses as a successful general in the Egyptian army. Because of his tremendous feats on the battlefield, Moses became an Egyptian hero. Since the Pharaoh's daughter had no children of her own, he also became a likely heir to the throne of Egypt. (See *Antiquities of the Jews*, trans. William Whiston [Grand Rapids, MI: Kregel Publications, 1960], book 2, chs. 9–10.)

Although we are not sure how Moses came to understand his responsibility to free the Israelites, Stephen implied that he at least partly understood this divine calling while still serving as an Egyptian prince. Stephen taught, "And when [Moses] was full forty years old, it came into his heart to visit his brethren the children of Israel. . . . For he supposed his brethren would have understood how that God by his hand would deliver them: but they understood not." (Acts 7:23, 25.)

While visiting the Hebrews, Moses fought with and killed an Egyptian and hid his body in the sand. The word *slew* that is used in the King James Version of the Bible is translated from the Hebrew word *nakhah,* which means "to beat down." This word was often used to describe personal combat between two soldiers. Elder Mark E. Petersen suggested several reasons why Moses may have killed the Egyptian:

> The historian Eusebius says that the slaying was the result of a court intrigue in which certain men plotted to assassinate Moses. In the encounter it is said that Moses successfully warded off the attacker and killed him. (Eusebius IX:27.)
>
> In the Midrash Rabbah, the traditional Jewish commentary on the Old Testament, it is asserted that Moses, with his bare fists, killed an Egyptian taskmaster who was in the act of seducing a Hebrew woman. This is confirmed in the Koran.
>
> Certainly there must have been good reason for Moses' act, and most assuredly the Lord would not have called a murderer to the high office of prophet and liberator for his people Israel. (*Moses: Man of Miracles* [Salt Lake City: Deseret Book Co., 1977], p. 42.)

Whatever the reason for killing the Egyptian, Paul made it clear that Moses did not just accidentally end up on the side of the Hebrews:

> By faith Moses, when he was come to years, refused to be called the son of Pharaoh's daughter;
>
> Choosing rather to suffer affliction with the people of God, than to enjoy the pleasures of sin for a season;
>
> Esteeming the reproach of Christ greater riches than the treasures in Egypt: for he had respect unto the recompence of the reward.
>
> By faith he forsook Egypt, not fearing the wrath of the king: for he endured, as seeing him who is invisible. (Hebrews 11:24–27.)

When Pharaoh sought to slay Moses, Moses fled Egypt and spent the next forty years serving as a humble shepherd while God prepared him to fulfill his divine mission of freeing the people of Israel.

God's guidance and direction is not restricted to major people and events—his guiding hand can be seen in the lives of all those who respond to the Spirit and desire to follow him. Chad Reeves was just such a person.

Less than a year following his baptism into the Church, Chad decided that he wanted to serve a mission. Because of his brief membership, he was not financially prepared to go, but his bishop assured him that a way would be provided if he would prepare himself spiritually.

Chad had served in the mission field for a month before he learned how his mission was being paid for. Shortly after he had expressed his concerns to the bishop, an elderly member of the ward named Sister Webb had approached the bishop with the desire to financially support a missionary. She had been saving her money all of her life so that she could go on a mission, but her health had deteriorated to the point that she could not serve. She wanted to use this money to help someone else; when she heard about Chad's situation, she was excited to pay for his mission.

Chad's heart was touched with Sister Webb's unselfish desire to support him in his missionary service, and they corresponded often throughout his mission. They began to feel very close to each other even though they had never met. In one especially meaningful letter, Sister Webb shared that she had always wanted to serve a mission and that her one desire was to live long enough to meet Chad personally. She indicated that her health was very poor and that she prayed daily that she would be able to hear firsthand about "their mission."

Chad had served fifteen months when the announcement was made that missions would be increased from eighteen months to two years. He was given the option of going home at the end of eighteen months or serving for a full two years. Sister Webb wrote and told him that she was more than willing to support him for the additional six months—and he was excited at the prospect—but as he prayed about it the Lord prompted him to go home after eighteen months. Even though Chad could not think of any reason why the Lord would want him to go home early, his mission president encouraged him to follow the promptings of the Spirit.

Chad visited Sister Webb the day after returning home, and

they spent many hours talking about "their mission." She was the very first person that Chad shared his mission experiences with. As Chad was leaving, Sister Webb took his hand and, with tears in her eyes, said that her prayers had been answered. She said that her one desire had been to meet him and hear about the mission. Now that desire had been fulfilled.

Chad was so overcome with love that he could not speak. They hugged one another and he left with tears streaming down his cheeks. The day before his homecoming address in his ward, Chad received a call from the bishop: Sister Webb had been killed in an auto accident, and the family wanted him to be a pallbearer at the funeral. As Chad thought about the time they had spent together, he understood why he had come home after eighteen months. The Lord was answering his daughter's humble prayers.

God is no respecter of persons. He loves each of us as much as he loves Moses, Chad, and Sister Webb. We all have important things to accomplish and spiritual desires that we would like to have fulfilled. As we strive to respond to the Spirit and to the word of God, we will receive the guidance that we desire so that we can play a meaningful role in the building of the kingdom of God.

21

The Call of Moses

EXODUS 3–4

The Lord promised Abraham that his descendants would be given the land of Canaan, but this promise was not fulfilled during his lifetime. One reason for this was that the people who possessed the land of Canaan were not yet ripe in iniquity (see Genesis 15:16). The process of becoming more wicked can be compared to the ripening of fruit. An apple will continue to ripen until it becomes totally rotten. When this happens with people, the scriptures refer to them as being full of iniquity or ripe in iniquity. Once a whole nation of people become completely rotten, they cut themselves off from God's guidance and protection.

Abraham was told that his seed would suffer affliction as slaves in another land for four hundred years. However, he was also promised that after this period of time his descendants would come out of this land "with great substance" and return to the land of Canaan (see Genesis 15:13–16). During these four hundred years, the inhabitants of the land of Canaan continued to degenerate spiritually until they sank into a fulness of iniquity.

Meanwhile, the Lord had been preparing Moses as the Israelites' prophet and deliverer. It was now time for Moses to receive his official call from the Lord.

As Moses was watching over his father-in-law's flock of sheep, in the land of Midian he noticed a bush that was burning but was not being consumed, so he turned aside to investigate "this great sight." God called to Moses out of the midst of the bush and told him to take off his shoes, since he was standing on holy ground. There was nothing special about the ground in and of itself, but the Lord's presence made it special. Things that are holy have been consecrated to God's service; Moses was soon going to be asked to consecrate the rest of his life to the Lord. The practice of removing the shoes as one enters holy places is practiced in our temples.

The Lord told Moses that he had seen the affliction of his people in Egypt and had come down to deliver them and to lead them to a good land—a land that was flowing with milk and honey. Everything went fine until the Lord told Moses he wanted him to return to Egypt and lead the Israelite people to freedom. Moses hesitated about accepting the call and asked, "Who am I, that I should go unto Pharaoh, and that I should bring forth the children of Israel out of Egypt?" (Exodus 3:11.)

Having lived in Egypt for forty years, Moses was well aware of the nation's great power and might. Even today, those who visit Egypt can't help but catch a vision of the mighty empire that once stood there. As my wife and I stood among the ancient pillars of the Karnak temple, we realized for the first time what great faith Moses must have had to walk into Pharaoh's court and tell him to release the Israelite slaves. Karnak is actually a whole city of temples that took about two thousand years to build and covers one hundred acres. One area of this complex is called the Hall of Columns and is the largest columnar structure ever built by man. It consists of 134 sandstone columns and covers an area of 56,000 square feet. The central columns stood sixty-nine feet tall and were thirty-three feet in circumference. They were so large that one hundred men could stand on the top of each pillar. As we stood in the middle of this huge temple complex, we discussed the fact that our beautiful Salt Lake Temple could be placed in a tiny corner of one of Karnak's many rooms.

Outside the Karnak complex are the remains of several sphinxes that used to line the two-mile avenue between Karnak and the temple of Luxor. Approximately 1,500 sphinxes originally lined this avenue, and, as I stood in the middle of the road, I wondered if Moses had walked down a similar road on his way to the king's palace.

Even if the majesty and might of the Egyptian empire did not cause Moses to hesitate about accepting the call, we must not forget that he was a wanted man in Egypt. He had fled forty years earlier in order to save his life. Whatever the reason for his hesitation, God knew that he was the right man for the job and promised Moses that he would not be alone.

To Moses' first question, "Who am I that I should go?" the Lord answered that he would be with him. The amount of talent or personal ability we have—or don't have—really doesn't matter if the Lord is with us, for we then tap into his great power and intelligence and can do whatever he calls us to do.

Moses was also concerned about being accepted by the Israelites and asked the Lord what he should say when the Israelites asked him who sent him. God's answer is an interesting one: "Thus shalt thou say unto the children of Israel, I AM hath sent me unto you" (Exodus 3:14). I AM was a name well known to the Israelites and is the English first person equivalent for YHWH or Jehovah, which meant HE IS. God refers to himself as I AM, and we call him Jehovah or HE IS. To the children of Israel, this name meant that God was there and that he would always be there.

Still fearing that the people would reject him, Moses said, "They will not believe me, nor hearken unto my voice: for they will say, The Lord hath not appeared unto thee" (Exodus 4:1). To bolster Moses' faith, the Lord gave him two signs that would show that he came from God.

The Lord told Moses to take the staff that he was holding in his hand (probably a shepherd's crook) and cast it on the ground. When he did so, it immediately turned into a serpent. Moses was then commanded to take it by the tail, and when he did so it became his staff again. The Lord may have chosen this particular sign because of an Egyptian custom. Most Pharaohs wore a metal cobra on their headdress as a symbol of their power. This sign would thus indicate God's great power. If the rod were a shepherd's staff, it would likely represent the Savior.

For the second sign, the Lord commanded Moses to place his hand inside his robe; when he withdrew it, his hand was leprous and as white as snow. When he put his hand in his robe and withdrew it again, the leprosy was gone. The Lord then told Moses that if Pharaoh refused to hearken to his words or to these two signs, he was to take water out of the river and pour it upon the dry land. The water would then turn to blood.

Moses still questioned his capabilities. He was not eloquent, he said, but was "slow of speech, and of a slow tongue" (Exodus 4:10; see also JST, Exodus 6:29). This could mean that Moses suffered from a mild speech impediment, or it may reflect the fact that he had not spoken the Egyptian language for forty years and had lost his mastery of the language. In either case, the Lord's answer is a promise to all of us as we accept his callings and strive to do his will. He said, "Who hath made man's mouth? or who maketh the dumb, or deaf, or the seeing, or the blind? have not I the Lord? Now therefore go, and I will be with thy mouth, and teach thee what thou shalt say." (Exodus 4:11–12.)

When Moses still wanted someone else to be sent in his place, God's anger was kindled: he promised Moses that Aaron would be a spokesman for him and sent him on his way. As we know, in spite of this slow beginning, Moses became one of the greatest prophets of all time.

Sometimes, as Moses did, we underestimate the great power the Lord can give us if we will but try to respond to his Spirit and live his gospel. This was illustrated well by a young returned missionary named Brett London. He was an English major and needed straight A's during his final three years of college in order to be accepted by the law school he desired to attend. He ended up in a writing class with a professor who "was on a personal crusade to combat grade inflation" and who expressed many antireligious feelings during class.

Brett spent two weeks writing and rewriting his first assignment until he was sure that he had an A paper. Much to his surprise and chagrin, he received a C grade instead. When he approached the professor about what was expected in order to receive an A, he was told that "only God gives A's."

The professor only gave them one week to fulfill the next assignment, but for Brett it was a week stuffed with Church commitments. Monday was a special home evening, and Brett had to spend Tuesday evening finishing his home teaching. He was responsible for conducting a Young Adult activity on Wednesday, and Thursday he had been assigned to speak in stake priesthood meeting. Friday was spent showing a friend from the mission field southern California, and all day Saturday Brett did yard work for an incapacitated family. Saturday evening was spent at the baptism and confirmation of a close friend.

This only left Sunday, as the paper was due Monday morning. Since Brett had promised the Lord that he would never do schoolwork on the Sabbath, he found himself arising early Monday morning to write his paper. He spent one hour brainstorming, another hour writing, and then had to turn the paper in without any revisions or corrections.

Brett had done his best but truly expected to receive a failing grade on the paper. A week later, before passing back the papers, the professor said, "Class, I suppose I have a reputation for being a hard grader. Well, I want you to know that today, for the first time in my teaching career, I have awarded a student an *A*-plus." The instructor then told the class that it was Brett's paper. As Brett looked back on this experience he wrote, "Perhaps the professor was right after all when he said, 'Only God gives *A*'s.'" (Brett G. London, "Only God Gives *A*'s," *Ensign*, March 1988, pp. 55–56.)

Moses, Brett, and Enoch all received strength from the Lord as they made the decision to place his work first in their lives. We cannot just ignore our responsibilities and expect God to do them for us, but when we are striving to keep the commandments and fulfill our callings in the Church, we invite into our lives the uplifting strength and influence of the Holy Ghost. Our abilities are increased and our talents multiplied, and we find ourselves able to accomplish things both in and out of the Church that are above our natural capabilities. We can trust in the Lord and accept calls that come to us, for he would never call us to a position that we cannot fulfill with his help.

22

The Ten Plagues

EXODUS 5–12

Moses' initial approach to Pharaoh was not a very happy or productive one. Pharaoh's reply to Moses was, "Who is the Lord, that I should obey his voice to let Israel go?" (Exodus 5:2.) He blamed Moses for slowing down the work that the Israelites had been given and decided that he would keep them too busy to listen to Moses. In the past the slaves had been given the necessary straw to make bricks, but Pharaoh commanded his taskmasters to make the people gather their own straw. In spite of this added burden, their required daily quota of bricks remained the same. The Israelite people blamed Moses for their increased workload and refused to hearken to his words.

Once again Moses expressed to the Lord his doubts about freeing Israel, but the Lord said, "The Egyptians shall know that I am the Lord, when I stretch forth mine hand upon Egypt, and bring out the children of Israel from among them" (Exodus 7:5). This knowledge of God's power would come to the Egyptian people as they suffered the effects of the ten plagues that were soon to be poured out upon them and their land. The purpose of these plagues, however, was not just to bring havoc on the people until they finally gave in and freed the Israelites. These plagues were established to demonstrate that God was more powerful than all of the counterfeit gods that were worshiped throughout Egypt and in many other parts of the world. Since many of the Egyptian customs and beliefs must have rubbed off on the Israelites during their 430 years of sojourn in Egypt, it was important that God's chosen people be reminded that there was but one true and living God.

The Egyptians worshiped many gods made of wood and stone, in both human and animal form, some of them representing powers of nature such as the Nile River, the sun, the moon, the sky, and the earth. God used the ten plagues to show both the Egyptians and the Israelites that his power was greater than any and all of the false gods worshiped in Egypt. Not only did the Egyptian gods fail to stop the Lord's power, but the Lord also used these impotent gods to bring torment and destruction upon the Egyptian people.

The first plague is a good example of what the Lord had in mind. I still remember flying over the land of Egypt and seeing the vegetation along the Nile River as a thin green line of color stretching through a vast land of sand and wilderness. As I looked out the plane's window, I realized that the Nile River truly was the lifeblood of Egypt. So it was at the time of Moses: the Egyptian people worshiped the Nile's life-giving water as the land's crucial source of fertility. When Moses turned the Nile's water into blood, God demonstrated that he was more powerful than Hopi, the Egyptian god of the Nile, and caused the river to bring ruin instead of prosperity. One of the serious side effects was that the fish quickly died, which meant that one of the people's most important food sources was taken from them.

When Pharaoh refused to respond positively to this plague, "Aaron stretched out his hand over the waters of Egypt; and the frogs came up, and covered the land of Egypt" (Exodus 8:6). These frogs were everywhere—even in the beds, ovens, and kneading troughs of the people. Once again God demonstrated his superior power over a god of Egypt, for frogs were considered a sign of fruitfulness and were worshiped as the goddess Heqt, who assisted in childbirth. Instead of fruitfulness, the frogs brought chaos and disease. Following this plague, Pharaoh said that he would let the Israelites go, but when God caused the frogs to return to the river or die, Pharaoh hardened his heart and went back on his word.

Aaron brought about the third plague by smiting the dust of the land with his rod, and the dust became lice throughout all the land of Egypt. Pharaoh's magicians told him that it was done by the "finger of God" and acknowledged God's great power, but Pharaoh still hardened his heart.

The fourth and fifth plagues were also direct strikes against the bogus gods of Egypt. The fourth plague consisted of swarms of flies that entered into the house of Pharaoh, his servants' houses, and all the land of Egypt. These flies did not bother the land of Goshen, where the Israelites lived, but instead destroyed the Egyptian lands. The Egyptians often used flies or beetles as symbols of the powerful sun-god Ra, one of their chief Deities. Once again, God used a symbol of one of the Egyptians' own gods to bring destruction and misery upon them.

The Egyptians worshiped many animals and animal-headed deities, including the bull-gods Apis and Mnevis, the cow-god Hathor, and the ram-god Khnum. The fifth plague was directed at these gods, and once again the Egyptian religion was rebuked and ridiculed. This plague brought disease and death on the cattle, horses, asses, camels, oxen, and sheep of the Egyptians. However, the Lord protected the Israelites so that none of their stock was affected.

The next three plagues—boils, hail mixed with fire, and locusts—brought even greater destruction upon the Egyptian people, yet Pharaoh still refused to let God's people go. By this time the Egyptian magicians and people were pleading with Pharaoh to release the Israelites, but he refused to budge.

The ninth plague was a plague of darkness, and it directly discredited Ra, the Egyptian sun-god. The sun was one of Egypt's chief deities, and for three days thick darkness covered the land. The scriptures indicate that this darkness was so thick that it could be felt, and that no one left their homes or saw another person until the darkness was lifted. During these three days of darkness, the children of Israel had light in their dwellings. Pharaoh still refused to soften his heart, and he told Moses that he would have him put to death if he saw his face again. This led to the plague that caused every Egyptian home to cry out in misery and sorrow, for the death of the firstborn struck every Egyptian family.

The Lord had already discredited most of the Egyptian gods, but, talking about the devastating plague of death that would soon be unleashed upon the Egyptian people, the Lord said, "Against all the gods of Egypt I will execute judgment: I am the Lord" (Exodus 12:12). The people prayed to their gods and asked them to protect their families, yet all of their gods were shown to be powerless to deliver them from the power of the Israelite God. The symbolism of the passover feast and how it pointed forward to the atonement of Christ will be covered in the next chapter. Suffice it to say here that this plague of death passed by all those who followed the Lord's directions and placed the blood of a lamb above their doors.

At midnight, the Lord "smote all the firstborn in the land of Egypt, from the firstborn of Pharaoh that sat on his throne unto the firstborn of the captive that was in the dungeon; and all the firstborn of cattle. . . . And there was a great cry in Egypt; for there was not a house where there was not one dead." (Exodus 12:29–30.)

The pain and grief were so intense that Pharaoh called Moses by night and told him to take his people and belongings and leave Egypt. God had told Moses earlier that the people would not leave Egypt empty-handed, and so it was. God told the people to ask the Egyptian people for gold and silver, for jewels of all kinds, and for fine clothing and other precious goods. The Lord then touched the hearts of the Egyptians, and they gave these things to the Israelites so that they left Egypt as a rich people. This followed Israel's law that they were to give gifts to any slaves that they released and was partial payment for the 430 years they had spent in the service of Egypt.

The scriptures indicated that six hundred thousand men (presumably aged twenty years and older) left Egypt in this exodus. This would mean that the total number of Israelites would be at least two million. Some feel that this number is high, but one thing is sure—Moses was faced with a responsibility of gigantic proportions as he led the Israelites into the wilderness. Just taking care of the food, water, shelter, and sanitation needs of this people would be overwhelming, but he was responsible for their spiritual needs as well. After four hundred years of dependence on Egypt, the people's faith and spirituality left something to be desired. Many other demonstrations of

God's power and the dying of the older generation would be necessary before the people were faithful enough to enter the promised land.

God has never quit demonstrating his power on behalf of his people. Sometimes his power comes in quiet ways as he removes venom and hate from an injured heart and replaces these poisons with peace and love. At other times he manifests his power by healing the sick, raising the dead, or controlling the elements so that injury or death is avoided. Many of the plagues at the time of Moses heaped destruction on the Egyptians yet avoided the Israelites. This principle is still in effect today. God can direct his power so that only those who are worthy to receive his blessings become the beneficiaries of his power. This was illustrated well in the lives of Darrell, Hjordis, and their two children.

Because of health problems, Darrell had been forced to change occupations, and he and his family were facing five months of no income. They prepared for this problem by selling their home. With the proceeds from this sale, along with their savings, they paid cash for a real fixer-upper house located on a half acre of property in a rural community

After many hours of hard work, they made the basement of the house barely livable. Their two children shared one small bedroom, and Darrell and his wife shared the other one. The floors were old pock-marked cement, and the interior doors were hung blankets. They bought a bathroom sink and toilet at a yard sale, and the bathtub was one that they had found abandoned in the backyard.

The main floor of the house was totally gutted and had become the home for several hives of bees. The stairs to the main floor consisted of several rickety ammunition boxes stacked on top of each other. Darrell installed a hot water heater, and his family was in the homemaking business again.

With a borrowed Rototiller and lots of muscle and sweat, the family turned the entire backyard into a vegetable and fruit garden. Their food storage, plus judicious budgeting of their remaining savings, looked to be just enough to keep the family eating until the garden could support them. They knew that when Darrell resumed work in the fall, it would take many months to catch up financially, so a bountiful harvest from their garden had become a necessity.

When everything sprouted in the garden and began to grow, they were quite pleased with how things were going. They felt good that they had been able to meet their financial challenge without help from any other source. They didn't have much, but it felt great to see their plan working. And work it did—until the advent of the grasshoppers.

The conditions had been just right that year for nature to produce grasshoppers in epidemic proportions. Their home was surrounded by fields filled with numerous kinds of grasses and weeds. These fields provided a perfect habitat for these hordes of insects with their voracious appetites. There were so many grasshoppers that, if a person didn't keep his mouth closed when passing through the fields, he would end up with an unwelcome breakfast. It seemed that hundreds of grasshoppers inhabited every few feet of ground.

When the weeds in the fields dried out, the grasshoppers discovered the green succulent plants in Darrell's garden, which immediately turned into a grasshopper cafeteria. Nothing they did slowed down the grasshoppers in any way. Any grasshoppers that were killed through spraying were quickly replaced by new recruits from the other side of the fence. It looked as if their much-needed vegetables were doomed to destruction, and they finally realized that they needed to turn to the Lord. They were reading the scriptures together when they ran across this promise, "And I will rebuke the devourer for your sakes, and he shall not destroy the fruits of your ground" (Malachi 3:11).

This promise had to do with the paying of tithing, and they had been full-tithepayers all of their lives. Darrell's family needed this promise to be fulfilled in their lives, and they needed it right away. Accordingly, they knelt in prayer as a family and pleaded with the Lord to protect their garden from the devouring grasshoppers. To make a long story short—He did! There were still just as many grasshoppers in the fields behind their home and in other gardens in their community, but their garden was left alone. Where hundreds of grasshoppers had been in their garden before, now there were only a few. It was as if there were an invisible high wall around their garden, and only a few grasshoppers could get over it. Their harvest was plentiful, and it fed them throughout the fall and winter and even into the next spring, when they were finally able to start catching up financially. Darrell and his family discovered that great blessings really did come when they humbled themselves and sought the power of the Lord.

Most members of the Church can share experiences of when the Lord has lovingly poured out his power on behalf of them and their loved ones. Obedience, humility, and prayer place us in a position to receive the great blessings that God desires to give us. Not only has God given us the gospel, the Atonement, prophets, the scriptures, and the gift of the Holy Ghost, but he also desires to bless us even further if we will but trust in him and realize the importance of inviting him into every portion of our lives.

23

The Lord Institutes the Passover

EXODUS 11–13

Nephi taught that "all things which have been given of God from the beginning of the world" symbolize Jesus and his atonement (2 Nephi 11:4). One of the greatest and most important of these symbols was the feast of the passover. It accompanied Israel's deliverance from bondage and symbolized the possible deliverance of all of us from sin. The feast of the passover was initiated as a reminder of the Israelites' protection from the tenth plague, and it was observed for over fifteen hundred years. Its symbolism pointed forward to the atonement of Christ just as the sacrament directs our thoughts and actions back to that profound event. Following are some of the passover procedures and what they represented:

The Lord's Instructions	What They Represented
Israel was in bondage to an evil power.	Men and women are in bondage to Satan and sin.
They were to kill a male lamb that was without spot or blemish.	Jesus is the Lamb of God. He lived a sinless life and therefore was without blemish.

The Lord's Instructions	What They Represented
No bones were to be broken in the sacraficial lamb.	The soldiers broke the bones of the thieves who were crucified with Christ, but none of Jesus' bones were broken.
The Israelites were promised the destroying angel would pass over all those homes with lamb's blood on their door posts. (Physical salvation.)	The blood of Christ that was spilled in the Garden of Gethsemane and on the cross saves all those who faithfully obey him.
They were to roast and eat the lamb until nothing of it remained.	We are to internalize the Atonement and make it an integral part of our lives. We should accept the Atonement completely, without reservations.
For seven days they were to eat unleavened bread only and were to have no leaven in their houses.	Leaven (yeast) was a symbol of corruption because it easily spoiled and turned moldy. It was also a symbol of pride, because it caused the dough to raise or puff up. We can benefit from the Atonement only if we avoid corruption and pride.
Even today, before celebrating the passover, many Jews search their homes and remove all leavened bread.	This symbolizes the need we all have of carefully searching our own lives for impurities and pride.
No uncircumcised person was to eat of the passover meal.	The blessings of the Atonement are reserved for those who make sacred covenants with God by becoming members of his earthly Church and kingdom.
Bitter herbs were eaten to show the bitterness of their bondage in Egypt.	Even more bitter than physical bondage is the spiritual bondage of sin.

The Lord's Instructions	What They Represented
They were to eat while standing with their loins girded, their shoes on, and their staffs in their hands. They were to eat in haste as if ready to leave Egypt at a moment's notice.	We need to be prepared to flee from sin and temptation as soon as it presents itself to us.
The death of the firstborn in each house in Egypt brought release and freedom to the Israelite people.	The death of Jesus, the firstborn son of God, brings release from sin and true freedom to all those who repent and follow him.

The last supper that Christ ate with his Apostles was also the last passover supper accepted by God. During this meal, the Savior replaced the passover with the sacrament, which likewise symbolically teaches and testifies of the Savior's atonement and of the special covenants we make at baptism.

The bread represents the body of Christ that was beaten and broken in our behalf. Jesus allowed himself to suffer all kinds of physical and emotional abuse so that he would be able to succor us in our times of distress and need. He then broke the bands of death and made it possible for all of us to be resurrected.

The water represents the blood of Christ that he willingly and lovingly shed both in the Garden of Gethsemane and on the cross. This blood was shed as Christ suffered for our sins. He did this out of love so that we would not have to suffer unless we refuse to repent and accept his gift. The suffering was so intense and excruciating that it caused Jesus to "tremble because of pain, and to bleed at every pore, and to suffer both body and spirit" (D&C 19:18).

The first promise we make to God when we partake of the sacrament is that we are willing to take upon us the name of Christ. We first made this promise at the waters of baptism when we became members of the Church of Jesus Christ. In effect, this promise means that we will do our best to live in such a way that others will see our good works and come to glorify God the Father and his Son, Jesus Christ (see Matthew 5:16.) As members of Christ's Church, we represent him throughout the world: almost everything we do can influence how others feel about him or his kingdom here upon the earth.

Another promise we make when partaking of the sacrament is that we will always remember the Savior and what he has done for us. The Hebrew word for *remember* means more than to just think about Christ. It means to go into action on his behalf. When God looked upon the Israelites in bondage and remembered the covenant he had made with Abraham, it meant that he was ready to act on their behalf and deliver them from Egypt. When we covenant to remember the Savior, we promise to do everything we can to spread his gospel and build his kingdom.

The third covenant we make when partaking of the sacrament is that we will keep the commandments he has given us. This is the best possible way of keeping the other promises of taking upon us his name and always remembering him. When we strive to keep God's commandments, people are attracted to his church and kingdom. They learn of his goodness and mercy, and they desire to make the atonement of Christ an integral part of their lives. There is nothing as important as obedience in bringing about our own salvation and the salvation of others.

If we keep these covenants, we are promised that we will always have the Spirit with us. The Spirit will sanctify our hearts, bridle our passions, and illuminate the course that we should follow. As we face the challenges of raising our families and making good choices in a world filled with sin, the Spirit will guide our thoughts and strengthen our actions. What a wonderful blessing can be given to us here upon the earth—being forgiven of our sins and receiving the companionship of the Holy Ghost! The seriousness with which we approach our sacramental covenants will greatly influence the amount of help and guidance we receive from the Spirit.

One father was taught the sacredness of the sacrament by his four-year-old daughter, Diana. She was sitting next to her father at church: "Diana sat reverently, enjoying the comfort of her father's arm holding her close to him. However, when the bishop stood up and announced the sacrament hymn, Diana gently lifted her father's arm from off her shoulder and placed it in his lap. Then she sat up straight and folded her arms. She looked over at her father and encouraged him to do the same.

Diana's message to her father was perfectly clear. She was telling him to turn his complete and total attention to the Savior." (L. Tom Perry, "Serve God Acceptably with Reverence and Godly Fear," *Ensign,* November 1990, p. 72.)

When we approach our sacramental covenants as Diana did, contemplate the great gift of the Atonement, and ask the Lord to help us keep our covenants, we will receive the guiding gift of the Spirit to comfort, direct, and strengthen us.

The twenty minutes or so that it takes to bless and pass the sacrament give us the opportunity to examine our lives and commune with our Father in Heaven. It can be a time of reflection on days gone by and of commitment for the days ahead. Specific goals can be set and promises made, and with a grateful and humble heart we can seek the help of the Lord in becoming a better person and a more productive servant. President David O. McKay said, "Meditation is one of the most secret, most sacred doors through which we pass into the presence of the Lord" ("The Lord's Sacrament," *Improvement Era,* May 1946, p. 271). The sacrament gives us an opportunity to take a mental and spiritual break from this busy world of ours and quietly communicate with our Father in Heaven.

The power that can accompany meaningful and committed sacrament observance was demonstrated by a soldier in Vietnam named Robert Hillman. For over three weeks he had been on constant patrol, chasing and being chased by the Viet Cong. He had just seen several of his friends killed and wounded and had been forced to take cover in a ditch from an enemy sniper's bullets. It had been several months since he had enjoyed any contact with the Church, and, as he was telling himself to hang on just a little longer, he heard someone whistling the hymn, "We Thank Thee, O God, for a Prophet."

As he listened to this familiar melody, his fears were calmed, and he quickly crawled over to the soldier who was whistling it. Robert asked him if he was worthy to administer the sacrament and he replied that he was. Robert knew that it was the Sabbath because of his calendar watch and he asked his fellow soldier if he would help him with the sacrament.

The two soldiers crawled out of the ditch and into the tall grass and bamboo, where they prepared to administer and partake of the sacred emblems of the Lord's sacrifice. A helmet became the table, and a white handkerchief the sacrament linen. They guarded each other while they took turns preparing and blessing the bread and water. Robert later recorded the powerful effect partaking of the sacrament had upon his hungry soul:

> Never in my life has the bread of the sacrament tasted so sweet and the water so pure as it did that day, nor has my soul been so strengthened by the ordinance. We clasped hands, then quickly crawled back to the protection of the ditch.
>
> . . . I never asked that soldier's name, nor he mine, but in those brief moments we forged a bond to last throughout eternity. That fellow Saint had rescued my soul from the horror and despair of war. Partaking of the sacrament in the jungle had brought me closer to the Lord than I had ever been before.
>
> Through a gospel ordinance we had found peace. (Robert K. Hillman, "Peace Amidst War," *Ensign*, April 1989, pp. 10–11.)

We cannot afford to be like many of the Israelites of Moses' day who participated in the outward ritualism of the ordinances but gave little thought to the symbolism and to the inner strength that could be gained from sincere and devout worship. As we approach the sacrament with the reverent attitude of Diana and the heartfelt need of Robert, our hungry souls will be filled and our spiritual thirst quenched. And, as the Lord has promised, we will receive his Spirit to be with us.

24

The Israelites
Enter the Promised Land

NUMBERS 13–14

JOSHUA 1–6

Preparatory to entering the promised land, Moses sent the leader of each of the twelve tribes of Israel into the land of Canaan to "spy out the land" (Numbers 13:16). They were to gather information that would help them obtain the land from those who currently lived there. They were also to report on the condition of the land and bring back examples of the fruit they found there.

After forty days, the spies returned with a dismal tale. They testified that the land was flowing with milk and honey, but ten of the spies said that the inhabitants were too strong to be defeated. They told of great walled cities and of people who were so large that, by comparison, they themselves felt like grasshoppers. Only two of the spies, Caleb and Joshua, were positive that with the Lord's help the land could be taken.

The Israelite people believed the ten spies and began to murmur against Moses and against God. They asked why the Lord had brought them to this land only to have their wives and children fall by the sword. They even decided to choose a captain to guide them back to the land of Egypt.

Joshua and Caleb stepped forth and bore testimony of the goodness of the land. They said, "If the Lord delight in us, then he will bring us into this land, and give it us; a land which floweth with milk and honey. Only rebel not ye against the Lord, neither fear ye the people of the land." (Numbers 14:8–9.)

Instead of responding favorably to the pleas of Joshua and Caleb, the Israelites decided to stone them. They were saved when the glory of the Lord appeared in the tabernacle before all the people. The Lord told Moses that because the people had rejected him and all the signs he had given them, they would not see the land that had been promised them. He said that all men aged twenty years and older, except for Joshua and Caleb, would die in the wilderness and that their children would then be given the land. The Lord indicated that this would take forty years, one year for each day that the spies had searched out the land. At the end of the forty years, Moses ordained Joshua as the next prophet-leader (Deuteronomy 34:9) and was taken by God into heaven. This left only Caleb and Joshua of the original men who had departed Egypt. Now the promises made to Abraham, Isaac, and Jacob could be fulfilled. Now their seed could be given the choice land that had been promised them.

Before Joshua led the people into the land of Canaan, he received promises and instructions from the Lord. God said to Joshua, "There shall not any man be able to stand before thee all the days of thy life: as I was with Moses, so I will be with thee: I will not fail thee, nor forsake thee" (Joshua 1:5). God told him to be strong and of good courage and, most important of all, to faithfully observe the laws that Moses had received so that the Lord could be with him and bless him. Emphasizing the importance of scripture study, even in the days of Joshua, the Lord said, "This book of the law shall not depart out of thy mouth; but thou shalt meditate therein day and night, that thou mayest observe to do according to all that is written" (Joshua 1:8). The Lord went on to promise Joshua that this would lead to prosperity and success.

Referring to this scripture, President Ezra Taft Benson said, "You must help the Saints see that studying and searching the scriptures is not a burden laid upon them by the Lord, but a marvelous blessing and opportunity. . . .

"The Lord was not promising Joshua material wealth and fame, but that his life would prosper in righteousness and that he would have success in that which matters most in life, namely the quest to find true joy." ("The Power of the Word," *Ensign,* May 1986, p. 81.)

Since all of us desire spiritual success and true joy, it behooves each of us to make regular scripture study an integral part of our lives. Through meaningful and consistent scripture study, we can come to know what God wants us to do and also come to better know the Lord.

Before crossing the River Jordan into the promised land, Joshua sent two men into Jericho as spies in order to evaluate the strengths and weaknesses of the city and of the people. They were seen going into the house of a harlot named Rahab. When the king of Jericho heard about the spies, he sent a message to Rahab telling her to bring the men out. For centuries, the people of the Near East have used the roofs of their homes for the purpose of drying grain or stalks, and Rahab was no exception. She hid the two spies among the stalks of flax that were drying on her roof and told the king's messengers that the men had already left. It was getting dark and she encouraged the messengers to quickly pursue the spies before they got away.

As soon as the king's men left, she went to the roof and bargained for the lives of her and her family. She told the spies that all of the people were "faint" because they knew the Lord had given the Israelites their land. She said that when the people had heard of the drying up of the Red Sea to help Moses' people escape, and of how easily the Israelites had defeated the two kings on the other side of the Jordan, their hearts had melted with fear. She then bore testimony and said, "The Lord your God, he is God in heaven above, and in earth beneath" (Joshua 2:11).

Rahab promised that she would help the spies escape if they would swear to her that she and her family would be saved when the city was destroyed. Her house was part of the city wall; after the men had promised that they would deal kindly with her, she attached a cord to the window on the outside of the wall and lowered them to the ground. Before leaving, the two men instructed her to gather her loved ones into her home and to tie a scarlet cord on the same window that she had just lowered them through. They promised her that all those in her house would be spared. The scarlet cord served a similar function to the blood of the passover lamb that the Israelites had spread on their doorposts. Whether it came from this story is not clear, but the early Christian church viewed a blood-colored cord as a symbol of Christ's atonement.

It looks as though Rahab was a true spiritual convert. She became a famous woman among the Israelites and was later honored in the New Testament for her faith (see Hebrews 11:31) and her good works (see James 2:25). Some Bible readers are somewhat troubled because they feel that the two spies should not have gone into the home of a harlot. It seems likely that the two men were chosen to be spies because they were righteous men and that they were directed by the Spirit to Rahab's home. There they not only found a person who was ready to accept the God of Israel but also obtained helpful information concerning the mind set of the people.

Two modern missionaries took part in a conversion experience similar to Rahab's. They knocked on a prostitute's door and were quickly invited in. When they realized the situation they were in, they started to leave—but the Spirit directed them to stay and teach her the gospel. They found out that she had been born to a prostitute mother and had been a prostitute herself since she was eight years old. She had never known anything else.

She was quickly converted to the gospel, and, during her baptismal interview, she was asked when she first knew the Church was true. She said that the moment the Elders entered her house she was told by the Spirit that whatever they told her would be the truth.

Both Rahab and the prostitute whom the missionaries taught demonstrate that the gospel is more than words on a page or symbolic ordinances. It is a real power that can literally change the innermost feelings and desires of those who respond to the Spirit. As we come to understand and appreciate how the Spirit works on the hearts of God's children, we find ourselves judging less and sharing the gospel more.

After the spies had given their report to Joshua, the Israelites moved their camp to the banks of the Jordan River.

There Joshua said to the people, "Sanctify yourselves: for tomorrow the Lord will do wonders among you" (Joshua 3:5). The Lord then said unto Joshua, "This day will I begin to magnify thee in the sight of all Israel, that they may know that, as I was with Moses, so I will be with thee" (Joshua 3:7). The Lord did this by splitting the Jordan River for Joshua, just as he had split the Red Sea for Moses.

The area of the Jordan River near Jericho was usually eighty to one hundred feet wide, but this was the time of the year when the river overflowed its banks. During this flood stage, the river often becomes a mile wide and very treacherous to cross. The priests who carried the ark of the covenant preceded the children of Israel into the river. As soon as their feet touched the water of the Jordan, the waters rose "up upon an heap" (Joshua 3:16). The priests then carried the ark of the covenant to the center of the riverbed and stayed there while all of the people of Israel passed over on dry ground. Since the ark signified the throne of God, this symbolized that the Lord was leading his people into the promised land and that he would remain in the place of danger until all of his people were safe. Just as with the ten plagues, God was also demonstrating his power over the heathen gods. The Canaanites worshiped Baal, whom they believed to be the king of the gods because he had triumphed over the sea god. Both this and the splitting of the Red Sea showed Israel and the Canaanites that God was the Lord over the waters.

When the Amorites and the Canaanites heard that the Lord had dried up the waters of the Jordan River, their hearts "melted, neither was there spirit in them any more" (Joshua 5:1). The effect of this great miracle also had a powerful and long-lasting effect on the Israelites, for "on that day the Lord magnified Joshua in the sight of all Israel; and they feared him, as they feared Moses, all the days of his life" (Joshua 4:14).

The day the people passed over the Jordan River was the day that the Lord had, many years before, set aside for the choosing of the passover lamb. Those males who had been born in the wilderness were circumcised, and the people celebrated the passover for the first time since leaving Egypt forty years before.

The Lord's plan for taking the city of Jericho seemed strange. The Israelites were told to march around the city once each day for six days. On the seventh day they were to march around the city seven times, and when the seven priests blew on their rams' horns, all of the people were to give a great shout. They were promised that if they followed these instructions perfectly, the mighty walls of Jericho would crumble and fall to the earth. Even though these instructions were unusual and even illogical, because the people had enough faith to obey the Lord the walls did fall and the city was captured.

Sometimes the Lord asks us to do things that seem unreasonable or illogical, but we will always receive the promised blessings if we trust in his word and follow his instructions. This important principle was illustrated in a story I once heard called "The Fox Hunter."

There was a fox hunter who had been very successful. As he grew older he decided to move to a warmer climate for awhile. As he was preparing to move, he was approached by a young man who wanted to take over his business and become a successful fox hunter.

The young man offered to pay the fox hunter well if he would sell him his shop and share with him the well-kept secrets that had made him such a successful hunter. The old hunter agreed and instructed the young man carefully in all the methods that he had learned through years of hunting.

The old man retired to the south for the winter, leaving a well-trained young man to follow in his footsteps. Upon his return, the old hunter asked the young man how he had fared. He was surprised when the young hunter sadly replied that he had not been able to catch a single fox. When the old man asked him if he had followed his instructions, the young man replied that he had not, because he had found a better way.

Sometimes we ignore God's commandments because we feel that we have a better way of gaining happiness and success. It is important that we come to understand that there is no better way than the Lord's way. When we follow his instructions, as Joshua and his people did in this instance, the blessings are sure. When we disregard the instructions of the Lord, we are as foolish as the young fox hunter and we forfeit our reward. We demonstrate true wisdom when we perceive that God is infinitely more intelligent than we are, and we therefore make the decision to trust in him and obey his commandments.

25

Three Hundred Against a Multitude

JUDGES 6–8

A few days before Christmas, a Cub Scout asked his father for two dollars so that he could make his father a present. When Christmas morning rolled around, the Cub Scout was more excited about the present he had made than he was about opening his own presents. In fact, the boy refused to open any of his presents until his Dad had unwrapped the precious gift that his son had lovingly made. The gift was a pencil holder for his father's office—made from a fruit jar that had been covered with brightly colored macaroni. The two dollars had been for the pencils and erasers that accompanied the gift. After seeing the pleasure with which his father accepted the gift, the boy turned to his own presents and eagerly began to open them.

Some time later, while thinking about this special Christmas, the father wrote: "In comparison with the bounteous gifts the Father bestows upon us—life, the Atonement, the gospel, prophets, scriptures, temples—our gifts to him are like jars covered with macaroni. It's the best we can do, and he accepts our efforts with pleasure. The realization of the difference between us and Him produces deep humility and blessedness."

(S. Michael Wilcox, "The Beatitudes: Pathway to the Savior," *Ensign*, January 1991, p. 20.)

When we sense the great need that we have for God's help and appreciate the bounteous blessings we enjoy because of him, we place ourselves in a position to receive greater help and favors from the Lord. As a matter of fact, one of the immense problems God faces is how he can bless us without our taking the credit ourselves and being filled with pride. The story of Gideon and his three hundred men is a good example of the great lengths God will go to help his children maintain their humility when he desires to bless them.

The children of Israel had done evil in the sight of God and had lost his protection and blessings. For seven years the Midianites and Amalekites had plundered the Israelites, robbing them of anything of value. The Midianites and Amalekites were wandering people who lived in the desert and stole from others. During harvest season they would sweep in from the deserts like swarms of grasshoppers and carry away all the grain and livestock they could find.

By the end of the seven years, the Israelites were suffering intensely from both hunger and humiliation. They had dug concealed caves and dens in the sides of the mountains to try to hide their goods, but their enemies had located most of their hiding places and had taken or destroyed the food they needed in order to stay alive. The scriptures indicate that no sustenance—"neither sheep, nor ox, nor ass"—was left for Israel.

Because they had nowhere else to turn, many people finally turned to God and appealed to him for relief from their suffering. Because they had forsaken him and turned to the worship of false gods, it had been difficult for them to admit their unrighteousness, overcome their pride, and truly humble themselves before the Lord.

The Lord sent a prophet to the Israelites to tell them why they had lost the Lord's protection. He reminded them of how God had delivered their forefathers from Egyptian bondage and had given them a promised land. He told them that God had warned them not to reverence the gods of the Amorites, but they had not obeyed his voice. The Lord then called a man named Gideon to free Israel.

At the time of his call, Gideon was threshing wheat inside a wine press in order to hide his wheat from the Midianites. An angel appeared to him and told him that the Lord would be with him and that he would be a mighty man of valor. When Gideon brought up the problems they were having with the Midianites, the Lord replied, "Go in this thy might, and thou shalt save Israel from the hand of the Midianites: have not I sent thee?" (Judges 6:14.)

Just as many humble men did who had preceded him, Gideon hesitated at first. He said, "Wherewith shall I save Israel? behold, my family is poor in Manasseh, and I am the least in my father's house." (Judges 6:15.)

The Lord promised that he would be with Gideon, gave him a sign that confirmed he had been called of God, and presented Gideon with his first assignment: Gideon was to destroy the altar of Baal that his father had built and then cut down the grove that stood next to it. The grove was a pole or tree that represented a heathen fertility goddess. Gideon was told to build an altar and use the wood from the grove in offering a burnt sacrifice to the Lord.

Because Gideon feared his father and the other men of the city, he waited until night to follow through on these instructions. The men of the city arose early the next morning and soon noticed that the altar of Baal had been destroyed and another altar built in its place. When they discovered that it was Gideon who had destroyed their altar, they commanded Joash, Gideon's father, to bring out his son so they could kill him.

Joash saved his son's life by saying, "Will ye plead for Baal? will ye save him? . . . if he be a god, let him plead for himself, because one hath cast down his altar." (Judges 6:31.) Gideon's confidence seemed to increase from this experience. When the Amalekites and Midianites gathered together to attack the Israelites, Gideon sent messengers throughout the land and gathered together a large army of his own.

The Lord was ready to help the people defend themselves, but he knew that, if he allowed them to go into battle with such a large army, they would take credit for the victory themselves. He wanted them to see his hand in their victory so they could develop the humility necessary for them to respond to him and his gospel. Therefore, he told Gideon to trim the size of the army.

Gideon was instructed to tell the men that anyone who was afraid should return to their homes. Twenty-two thousand men departed, which left Gideon with an army of ten thousand men. The Lord said to Gideon, "The people are yet too many" (Judges 7:4). Gideon was instructed to lead his army to a source of drinking water. All those who drank of the water by cupping the water in their hands and then lapping the water with their tongues were to remain; all those who knelt down to drink were to return home. Three hundred men lapped from their hands, and 9,700 men were dismissed from the army.

The Midianites and the Amalekites were camped in a valley "like grasshoppers for multitude; and their camels were without number, as the sand by the sea side for multitude" (Judges 7:12). God told Gideon that Israel would be saved from this enormous army by his three hundred men.

That night the Lord told Gideon that it was time for his small army to attack. He said that if Gideon was afraid, he should take his servant and sneak down close to the Midianite army; there he would hear something that would give him the courage and strength to attack.

Gideon and his servant overheard one of the enemy soldiers explain a dream that troubled him. He had dreamed of a cake of barley bread that tumbled into the host of Midian. This barley bread came into a tent and smote it until the tent fell and was overturned. The soldier listening to the dream said this meant that God had delivered all of the hosts of Midian into the hands of Gideon.

After listening to this conversation, Gideon returned to his camp to worship the Lord and prepare his men for battle. According to the Lord's direction, his army was divided into three groups; each man was given a trumpet and a pitcher with a lamp inside of it. Normally only a small portion of an army would carry trumpets.

After surrounding the Midianites on three sides, Gideon's men blew their trumpets, broke the pitchers so that the lamps were visible, and yelled, "The sword of the Lord, and of Gideon" (Judges 7:20). Because it was the middle of the night and the enemy soldiers were coming out of a deep sleep, they became afraid and confused—in total panic, they fought against each other! They then fled from what they supposed to be an unbeatable foe. Israelite men gathered from throughout Israel and pursued after the Midianites. The Midianite army was destroyed, and Israel enjoyed peace for the next forty years.

When the men of Israel asked Gideon to rule over them, he said, "I will not rule over you, . . . the Lord shall rule over you" (Judges 8:23). By doing this, Gideon emphasized that the Lord, not him, had won the battle for them. Gideon decided to use the spoils of war to honor God's part in the victory. He asked the soldiers to give him all of the gold jewelry they had removed from the dead soldiers. Gideon used the gold to make a new ephod that was worn by the chief priest in Israel. The purpose was to remind the people of God's great gift of freedom, but instead the people worshiped the ephod as an idol and placed their hearts on it instead of God. As soon as Gideon died, the people returned to the worship of Baal.

Although the Israelites at the time of Gideon had difficulty developing the humility that leads to divine guidance and spiritual growth, many others have learned to appreciate the Lord's hand in their lives. President Heber J. Grant once related an experience that helped him develop humility in his life.

Heber J. Grant became president of the Tooele Stake while still a young man. In his maiden speech, he ran out of ideas in just seven and one-half minutes. Later that night he heard someone say, "Well, it is a pity if the General Authorities of the Church had to import a boy from the city to come out here to preside over us that they could not have found one with sense enough to talk ten minutes."

The next three speeches he gave were just as short, with one of them only lasting five minutes. His next speech was in a small town named Vernon. When he arrived at the log meetinghouse, it was crowded with ward members. President Grant had taken two other brethren with him to do the preaching, as he expected that he would not be able to speak longer than five or six minutes. Instead he talked for forty-five minutes with great ease and really enjoyed himself. He recognized the inspiration of the Lord, and that night he shed tears of gratitude as he thanked the Lord for blessing him with His Spirit.

The following Sunday he was scheduled to speak in Grantsville, which was the largest town in Tooele County. He stood up with great confidence and told the Lord that he was planning on taking about forty-five minutes. Five minutes later he had run out of things to say and was so nervous he was perspiring.

Following the meeting, President Grant walked two or three miles until he reached the farthest haystack in Grantsville. There he knelt down and asked the Lord to forgive him of his pride and conceit. He made a pledge to the Lord that he would never stand before an audience again without first asking for the Lord's Spirit to be with him. He also pledged that he would not take credit in the future for anything that he said. Many years later, after repeating this story, President Grant testified that he had kept this promise. (See Heber J. Grant, "Honoring Dr. Karl G. Maeser," *BYU Quarterly,* November 1934, pp. 24–26.)

Very few things are more beneficial to us than developing a recognition of and an appreciation for the help and guidance that we receive from God. A deep sense of gratitude keeps the channel open between us and God, and we need his guidance every single day of our lives. Jesus often prayed for guidance from his Father, and so must we if we are to be successful parents, give effective Church service, and help those around us draw closer to our Father in Heaven. Without the help of our Father in Heaven, we have little to offer. With his help, we can successfully fulfill our many responsibilities and eventually become like him.

26

Samson Rejects His Call

JUDGES 13–16

A brief discussion of the judges of Israel can help in our under-standing of Samson and his role as a judge. When Joshua died, national spirit died and tribal loyalty replaced national loyalty. The judges were men (except in the case of Deborah) who held lead-ership positions during the period between Israel's conquest of Canaan and the reign of the kings. This period of Old Testament history was characterized by faithlessness and idolatry. During these four hundred years, a cycle of apostasy was repeated many times, generally according to the following pattern:

1. Peace and prosperity.
2. Pride.
3. Wickedness.
4. Destruction and bondage.
5. Humility and prayer.
6. Deliverance.
7. Repetition of the cycle, beginning with peace and prosperity.

The judges became leaders by either self-appointment, the request of the Israelite people, or the Lord's designation. They were more like heroes, champions, or deliverers than what we think of as judges today. Sometimes there was no judge in

Israel, and other times more than one judge may have ruled contemporaneously in different parts of Canaan.

Many judges did not possess great spiritual qualities but were chosen instead as military leaders to deliver Israel from her enemies. Even though the Lord aided some of the judges in battle, he did not necessarily approve of all of their actions. This is especially important to remember as we study Samson's life.

A few statements in the scriptural account of Samson are inconsistent with basic gospel principles. W. Cleon Skousen suggested that one reason for this is that periods of apostasy do not usually produce good historians, and that "there is not the same sense of sacred responsibility associated with the keeping of records as that which prevails during a period when men are in close communication with God."

Referring to these scriptural conflicts in the account of Samson, the author said:

> The unknown writer who left us the history of Samson seemed anxious to present him as a great hero of Israel whom God favored in spite of his apostasy. The author may have thought that by taking this approach he was doing a favor to Samson. But it was certainly no favor to God. It made the Lord a partner to all the stupid antics of a wilful, defiant spirit who had abandoned his calling and betrayed his God. (*The Third Thousand Years* [Salt Lake City: Bookcraft, 1964], p. 567.)

Samson had been foreordained to do great things and was born with tremendous promise and potential, but the scriptures clearly reveal that he used the strength God had given him for his own self-indulgence and failed to live up to his calling and covenants.

Joseph Smith taught that "every man who has a calling to minister to the inhabitants of the world was ordained to that very purpose in the grand council of heaven before this world was" (*History of the Church,* 6:364). We must not confuse foreordination with the false doctrine of predestination. When we were foreordained, certain promises, blessings, and powers were bestowed upon us, but these things will only come to pass if we are faithful and obedient. Joseph Smith was foreordained to restore and build the latter-day kingdom, yet God warned him that, "because of transgression, if thou art not aware thou wilt fall" (D&C 3:9).

The same is true for each of us. Elder Neal Maxwell said that "foreordination is like any other blessing—it is a conditional bestowal subject to our faithfulness." He taught that foreordination "foresees but does not fix the outcome." ("A More Determined Discipleship," *Ensign,* February 1979, p. 71.)

Talking to the youth, Elder Harold B. Lee said: "I fear there are many among us who because of their faithfulness in the spirit world were 'called' to do a great work here, but like reckless spendthrifts they are exercising their free agency in riotous living and are losing their birthright and the blessings that were theirs had they proved faithful to their calling. Hence as the Lord has said, 'There are many called but few are chosen.'" (*Youth and the Church* [Salt Lake City: Deseret News Press, 1945], pp. 175–76.)

With this background, we may be better prepared to understand Samson's life. Hopefully, as we study his life, we can identify problems and attitudes that caused him to falter; furthermore, we will gain some insights that can help us succeed in our own callings.

The children of Israel had been in bondage to the Philistines for forty years when Samson was born. Before his birth, an angel of the Lord appeared to Samson's mother, who was barren, and told her that she would bear a son. She was instructed that she should not drink wine or strong drink nor eat any unclean thing from the time of her conception. The angel indicated that Samson should never cut his hair and that he should be a Nazarite even while yet in his mother's womb.

The meaning of the Hebrew word for Nazarite is "to be dedicated or separated." Those people who vowed that they would dedicate their lives and actions to God were known as Nazarites. Usually this vow was given for a certain period of time, but God wanted Samson to dedicate his whole life to God's service. The angels suggested that Samson had been foreordained to "begin to deliver Israel out of the hand of the Philistines" (Judges 13:5). Samson's parents felt the great weight of raising a son who could affect the lives of all Israelites and asked the angel what they should do to help their future son fulfill this great calling. The angel answered their questions and ascended into heaven in a miraculous way.

After Samson was born, the Lord blessed him with great physical strength so that he would be able to fulfill his foreordained mission. This strength, like all gifts that we receive from God, was to be used under God's direction for the fulfilling of his purposes and for the blessing of his people. This was not generally what Samson did. Elder Mark E. Petersen wrote:

> Yes, Samson was strong in a physical way. But he was yet a weakling. . . . To a large extent, he was a failure in life. . . . He refused to control himself. . . . One compromise after another added to his weakness of purpose. His desire to be as other men blinded him to his responsibility and cheapened in his eyes the sanctity of his covenants. The more his resolution weakened, the further he sank into the ways of worldliness until at last he surrendered completely. (*Your Faith and You* [Salt Lake City: Bookcraft, 1953], pp. 243–46.)

One of the first scriptural indications of Samson's spiritual weakness was his desire to marry out of the covenant. Elder Bruce R. McConkie stated that "the most important things that any member of The Church of Jesus Christ of Latter-day Saints ever does in this world are: 1. To marry the right person, in the right place, by the right authority; and 2. To keep the covenant made in connection with this holy and perfect order of matrimony." (*Mormon Doctrine,* 2nd ed. [Salt Lake City: Bookcraft, 1966], p. 118.)

Covenant marriage was stressed just as much in Samson's day as it is today, if not more so, yet Samson wanted to marry out of the covenant. Samson told his parents that he had seen a Philistine woman he wanted to marry, and asked his father to make the arrangements. Samson's answer to their question of why he didn't marry a covenant person instead of disobeying the counsel of God reveals the selfish and uncontrolled nature of Samson. He said simply, "Get her for me; for she pleaseth me well" (Judges 14:3). In Hebrew, this expression is similar to several phrases that indicate that Samson usually did what he wanted to do with little concern for whether it conflicted with the word of God.

Most of the recorded accounts of Samson's impressive physical accomplishments seem to indicate that he very seldom fought for Israel but rather used his strength for his own self-indulgence. He killed thirty innocent men so that he could use their clothes to pay off a silly bet he had made. He tied firebrands to the tails of foxes or jackals and burned down the crops of the Philistines because he was upset at his wife and father-in-law.

Even though Samson had left his wife, when the Philistines killed her in retribution for their fields being burned, he vowed revenge and "smote them . . . with a great slaughter" (Judges 15:8). When Samson killed a thousand men with the jawbone of an ass, instead of expressing sorrow or regret, he seemingly bragged about his great feat. After spending the night with a harlot, Samson ripped off the huge city gates and carried them to the top of a hill. He knew some enemy soldiers were waiting to kill him, and perhaps this was his way of showing off his great strength.

Anger, jealousy, selfishness, revenge, lust, and immorality are all foreign to the Spirit of the Lord, yet three different times the scriptures say that the Spirit of the Lord came upon Samson and apparently strengthened him to do such deeds. Since we know that the help of the Spirit is usually obtained through righteousness, many readers question how Samson could have enjoyed the Spirit in these instances. Because this phrase is only used when referring to Samson's demonstrations of great courage and physical strength, "perhaps when the author of Judges used the phrase 'the Spirit of God,' he did not use it as we do today but rather more in the way that we would now use the phrase 'spiritual gift.' Samson's gift was strength, and each time he used that gift in a remarkable manner, the writer of the scripture gave credit to the Lord, the true source of the gift, by saying 'the Spirit of the Lord' came mightily upon him." (Old Testament Student Manual, p. 260.)

Finally, however, Samson lost both the Spirit of the Lord and his gift of strength. This came about through Samson's immoral association with Delilah. After lying to her several times about the source of his strength, Samson finally gave in to her daily pressuring and told her of his Nazarite vow. He said that his strength would be lost if his hair was shaved from his head. The sad thing is that Samson may have come to believe that the source of his power was his hair. His strength really came from God through his Nazarite oath, which was symbolized outwardly by his hair. The shaving of his hair was the final step in a long line of betrayed and broken vows, and God finally completely withdrew both his Spirit and Samson's special gift of strength.

Samson was so out of tune with the Spirit of the Lord that he knew not "that the Lord was departed from him" (Judges 16:20). Even though his hair had been cut, he still thought that he had his great strength and went out to do battle with his enemies. The Philistines did not want to kill him but wanted to "afflict him" (Judges 16:5) and humiliate him, so they captured him, put out his eyes, and took him to prison.

Thousands of Philistines gathered together to celebrate Samson's capture and to offer a great sacrifice to Dagon their god. They felt that the taking of Samson demonstrated that their god was more powerful than Samson's God. Not only were they making sport of Samson but were also degrading Jehovah and his people. Because of this, God gave Samson the strength to pull down the heathen temple. With this one powerful act, Samson killed more Philistines than he had throughout his life, yet even this final deed was performed for the wrong reason. Samson didn't request this last act of strength to demonstrate the power of God, or because he felt offended that the Philistines would insult God, or because he wanted to help the people. He asked God for the strength to pull down the temple so he could avenge himself on the Philistines for poking out his eyes.

Samson's pulling down the temple was a great testimony of Jehovah's power, but how much more effective Samson would have been if he had used daily his great power in freeing his people and in building up the kingdom of God. It was another hundred years before the people finally became free.

Each of us can receive the power of God in our lives as we strive to keep the commandments and fulfill our special callings from the Lord. Talking about our day, President Ezra Taft Benson said:

Each day the forces of evil and the forces of good enlist new recruits. Each day we personally make many decisions showing the cause we support. The final outcome is certain—the forces of righteousness will finally win. But what remains to be seen is where each of us personally, now and in the future, will stand in this battle—and how tall we will stand. Will we be true to our last days and fulfill our foreordained missions?

Great battles can make great heroes and heroines. You will never have a better opportunity to be valiant in a more crucial cause than in the battle you face today, and in the immediate future. Some of the greatest battles you will face will be fought within the silent chambers of your own soul. (Dedication: Boise Institute of Religion Building, Sunday, November 20, 1983.)

We live in a time of great opportunity. Thousands and millions of people are searching for the truth and for someone to guide them to the Savior and the peace that we all seek. President Wilford Woodruff taught that, out of the hundreds of millions of people on the earth, "we were chosen to come forth in this day and generation and do the work which God has designed should be done" (*Journal of Discourses* 21:193). Not only is it a great responsibility but also a wonderful blessing to be involved in helping a people prepare for the Savior's second coming. We bring with us into this life not only the traits and strengths that we developed previously but also foreordained powers and opportunities to help build the kingdom of God. As we live the gospel and respond to the Spirit, we will receive the direction and power that we need to fulfill our premortal and mortal callings, and we will perform an important service in the salvation of those around us.

27

Speak, for Thy Servant Heareth

1 SAMUEL 1–4

Much of the story of Samuel, Eli, and Eli's sons centers around the portable tabernacle that housed the ark of the covenant and represented the place where God came to speak to his people. The law of Moses required that three times a year all Israelite males present themselves before the Lord at the tabernacle, where they would worship through prayer and sacrifice.

Elkanah was a righteous Israelite who faithfully performed this responsibility. At least once a year, he would take his family with him. Elkanah had two wives: Hannah and Peninnah. Peninnah had children, but Hannah was barren. Every year when Elkanah's family would travel to the tabernacle, Peninnah would ridicule Hannah because "the Lord had shut up her womb" (1 Samuel 1:5). Hannah would become so upset that she could not eat and would spend much of her time crying.

This yearly trip to the tabernacle may very well have been to celebrate the festival called the Feast of Tabernacles. If so, this would be especially difficult for Hannah because it specifically celebrated with joy and feasting God's generous blessings on the year's crops and harvest. During this festive occasion, Hannah's deep sorrow because of her own barrenness would have been even more poignant. Even though Elkanah showed great love to Hannah, he could not comfort her.

After years of sorrow, Hannah went to the tabernacle "in bitterness of soul, and prayed unto the Lord, and wept sore" (1 Samuel 1:10). She vowed to the Lord that if he would remember her and give her a male child, once she had weaned him she would give him to the Lord. As mentioned in previous chapters, to remember was more than to simply recall that Hannah existed. She was asking the Lord to go into action on her behalf and give her a son.

Hannah spoke only in her heart; even though she mouthed the words with her lips, she did not say the words aloud. Eli, the high priest as well as a judge, thought she was drunk and rebuked her. When Hannah explained that she was filled with grief and was praying for a blessing from the Lord, Eli said to her, "Go in peace: and the God of Israel grant thee thy petition that thou hast asked of him" (1 Samuel 1:17).

Hannah had such great faith that her sadness was immediately replaced by hope and joy. The Lord did remember Hannah, and she had a son whom they named Samuel. In Hebrew, the name *Samuel* means "heard of God," and Hannah knew that her son was a gift from the Lord.

In Old Testament times, since there was no way to keep milk from spoiling, mothers usually nursed their children for up to three years. So Samuel was approximately three years old when Hannah took him to the temple and presented him to Eli. She told Eli, "For this child I prayed; and the Lord hath given me my petition which I asked of him: therefore also I have lent him to the Lord; as long as he liveth he shall be lent to the Lord." (1 Samuel 1:27–28.) Each year after this, when Hannah would come with her husband to offer sacrifice, she would visit with her son and give him a coat she had made him.

What great faith, love, and trust in the Lord were represented by Hannah's willingness to leave her young child in the hands of Eli and have him raised in the tabernacle complex! (The Scriptures suggest, with their references to doors and sleeping quarters, that the tabernacle at this time was adjacent to some type of living compound.) Because of her willingness to keep the promise she had made the Lord, he blessed Hannah with three more sons and two daughters.

After leaving her son at the tabernacle, Hannah sang praises and rejoiced in the Lord. She illustrates true humility and gratitude, for the supreme source of her joy was not in Samuel but in God, who answered her prayer and made Samuel's birth possible. Sometimes we get so caught up in enjoying our blessings that we forget to appreciate the giver of them.

Samuel grew up in the shadow of the tabernacle and ministered to the Lord under the direction of Eli the priest. While Samuel increased in faith and obedience, Eli's sons did just the opposite. The scriptures indicate that their hearts were filled with wicked and base desires and that they knew not the Lord. In Old Testament usage, to "know" the Lord was not just to intellectually know who he was but rather to enter into fellowship with him—to serve him and receive guidance and inspiration from him. Because the thoughts and actions of Eli's sons were unrighteous, they performed many wicked acts as they served as priests in the holy sanctuary of the Lord.

In those days it was customary for priests to receive part of each sacrifice to take care of their personal needs. After the burnt offering had been made to the Lord, the priest would randomly thrust a three-pronged fork into the meat and "all that the fleshhook brought up the priest took for himself" (1 Samuel 2:14). This was to be a voluntary offering to the priest by those who worshiped at the tabernacle.

Eli's sons, however, took their portion by force. They even placed themselves before the Lord by demanding their portion—often the best portion—before the sacrifice had been made to the Lord. They said that they did not want their meat cooked or sodden, but instead demanded it raw. If any man asked to burn the fat (make their burnt offering to God) before the priests took their share of the meat, Eli's sons would say, "Thou shalt give it me now: and if not, I will take it by force" (1 Samuel 2:16). The sin of Eli's sons was very great, for they "abhorred the offering of the Lord" (1 Samuel 2:17).

Eli's sons also lay with the women that assembled at the door of the tabernacle. This combination of worship and immorality was reminiscent of the religious prostitution performed at the Canaanite sanctuaries. It was an abomination to the Lord and a desecration of his house. Because Eli's sons were priests, their actions led others to transgress as well.

When Eli heard of the things that his sons were doing, he scolded them, but they "hearkened not unto the voice of their father" (1 Samuel 2:25). Because Eli's sons "made themselves vile" and Eli "restrained them not," the Spirit of the Lord was withdrawn from Eli (1 Samuel 3:13). He was told that the leadership of Israel would be given to another—one not of his family. He was also told that his two sons would both die the same day. The Lord explained that when Eli continued to let his sons minister in the tabernacle, he desecrated the Lord's sacrifice and offering and honored his sons above the Lord.

While these things were taking place in Eli's family, Samuel grew "in favour both with the Lord, and also with men" (1 Samuel 2:26). The scriptures state that there was no open vision in Israel and that the "word of the Lord was precious in those days" (1 Samuel 3:1). The fact that very little revelation was being received in Israel is no surprise: this had been the case for the past four hundred years, throughout the reign of the judges. The lack of revelation, however, was about to come to an end.

One night, while Samuel was still a child (Josephus says twelve years old), the Lord called him. It was in the early morning hours, and, when Samuel heard his name called, he answered, "Here am I" and ran to see what Eli wanted. Eli told him that he had not called him and instructed him to go back to bed.

Once again the Lord called Samuel, and once again, because this was his first experience with direct revelation, he did not realize who was speaking. After Samuel came to Eli for the third time, Eli finally perceived that it was the Lord who was calling Samuel. He told the boy that the next time he heard his name called, he should answer, "Speak, Lord; for thy servant heareth" (1 Samuel 3:9). Samuel followed these instructions and received the Lord's guidance and information. As part of this revelation the Lord told Samuel that Eli had sinned because his "sons made themselves vile, and he restrained them not" (1 Samuel 3:13).

Samuel continued to grow, and the Lord was with him insomuch that the Lord did "let none of [Samuel's] words fall to the ground" (1 Samuel 3:19). Because Samuel received from God the words he taught, all of his words came to pass and all of

Israel knew that he was a prophet. Once again, revelation and the word of the Lord were taught in Israel.

Following these events, Israel went out to battle against the Philistines. When the Israelites saw that they were losing the battle, they said, "Let us fetch the ark of the covenant of the Lord out of Shiloh unto us, that, when it cometh among us, it may save us out of the hand of our enemies" (1 Samuel 4:3). They remembered the ark's presence at notable victories in the past and were attempting to secure the Lord's presence in their battle. The problem was that they believed that the Lord's presence with the ark was guaranteed. They had embraced the pagan notion that God is identified with the symbol of his presence and that God's blessings could automatically be gained by manipulating the symbol. That the Philistines also believed this is evident, for when they saw the ark of the covenant, they were afraid and said, "God is come into the camp" (1 Samuel 4:7).

One of the most basic gospel principles is that all blessings are obtained through obedience to God's laws (see D&C 130:20–21). Even though we don't have the ark of the covenant, we sometimes make the same mistake the Israelites made. This false idea that God automatically accompanies certain things that represent him can surface in numerous ways. For instance, we know that God works through his priesthood and blesses people through priesthood ordinances. Yet worthiness is still a prerequisite if we desire the blessings of ordinances such as administering to the sick, partaking of the sacrament, baptism, temple endowments, and temple marriage. None of these ordinances automatically guarantee us the Spirit of the Lord or the promised blessings. Only through righteousness and service do we receive these blessings.

Because the Israelites were not worthy of the Lord's help, this battle with the Philistines produced a great slaughter in the Israelite ranks. Thirty thousand of them were killed, including Eli's two sons, and the Philistines captured the ark of the covenant. When Eli heard this news, he fell backwards off his bench and broke his neck. Thus ended Eli's forty-year reign as judge.

Samuel became the last judge of Israel. He spent the rest of his life striving to help the Israelite people forsake their false gods and turn to the Lord. Under the Lord's direction, he anointed Saul to be the first king of Israel.

We can learn several important lessons from this story of Samuel, Eli, and Eli's sons. One is the importance of listening and responding to the voice of the Spirit. Just as Samuel did, we need to learn how to recognize the promptings of the Holy Ghost. The Spirit speaks in a "still small voice" (1 Kings 19:12) and "does not get our attention by shouting or shaking us with a heavy hand. Rather it whispers. It caresses so gently that if we are preoccupied we may not feel it at all. . . . Occasionally it will press just firmly enough for us to pay heed. But most of the time, if we do not heed the gentle feeling, the Spirit will withdraw and wait until we come seeking and listening and say in our manner and expression, like Samuel of ancient times, 'Speak [Lord], for thy servant heareth.'" (Boyd K. Packer, "The Candle of the Lord," *Ensign*, January 1983, p. 53.)

One young man who put off responding to the Spirit's promptings has regretted it ever since. As he drove down the street one night, he saw some teenagers performing some pranks that he knew could lead to injury. The Spirit prompted him to approach them and encourage them to stop their actions, but he was in a hurry. He knew that he would be back that way in just a few minutes, so he decided that if they were still engaged in their dangerous escapades when he returned, he would try to put a stop to their actions. He returned just in time to see one of the teenagers hit by a car and killed. He has never put off responding to the Spirit of the Lord since that time.

Many times we do not know why the Spirit prompts us to do certain things, but we can have confidence that it is for the best of both ourselves and others. President Harold B. Lee had an experience as a young boy that illustrates this principle. He was out on a farm waiting for his dad to finish some work so they could go home. As he was manufacturing things to do, he noticed some old sheds and dilapidated buildings across the fence on his neighbor's yard. He decided it would be fun to explore these buildings and was climbing over the fence when he heard a voice say, "Harold, don't go over there." He looked all around to see who had spoken, but no one was in sight. He then realized that the Lord was watching over him and warning him of an unseen danger. He never found out what this danger was, but he learned to trust in the promptings he received from the Spirit. (See "Don't Go Over There," *New Era*, March 1973, p. 12.)

A great lesson negatively taught by Eli and his sons is the importance of properly disciplining our children. President Spencer W. Kimball taught that "discipline is probably one of the most important elements in which a mother and a father can lead and guide and direct their children. It certainly would be well for parents to understand the rule given to the priesthood in section 121. Setting limits to what a child can do means to that child that you love him and respect him. If you permit the child to do all the things he would like to do without any limits, that means to him that you do not care much about him." (*The Teachings of Spencer W. Kimball,* ed. Edward L. Kimball [Salt Lake City: Bookcraft, 1982], p. 341.)

Sometimes we are afraid that our children will be upset with us, so we back off from our responsibilities. If we discipline our children properly, the time will come when they will thank us for the love and direction that we gave them through their important learning and growing years. Ardeth G. Kapp, who served as general president of the Young Women, shared an experience that depicts this well:

> I remember one evening years ago, while attending a Sunday School party, I looked at the clock, and it was past the time I was told to be home. Just then a knock came on the door. I was horrified—my dad had come after me. I felt humiliated in front of my friends. I thought I wanted to die. I was not pleasant with my dad; disobedience never makes one pleasant.
>
> A few years later, my friends and I were driving home from a dance across an Indian reservation, ten miles from any shelter. It was 40 degrees below zero, and the windchill continued to lower the temperature. A few miles farther into the blizzard, we discovered that there was no heat in the car. Then the car froze up and would not run. We came to a slow stop. We watched the snow swirling in front of us only until the winds quickly froze over. We were quiet and sober as we contemplated our fate—our lives were in danger. The silence was broken as a friend in the backseat asked, "How long do you think it will be before your dad will get here?"
>
> Why do you think they thought my dad would come?

One time I had thought I wanted to die because he had come after me. This time we lived because my dad came through the blizzard to save my life and the lives of my friends. This time I was pleasant with my dad—pleasant and very grateful. ("Young Women Striving Together," *Ensign*, November 1984, pp. 96–97.)

Eli's sin of failing to restrain his sons was even more serious because he allowed them to continue desecrating the holy sanctuary with their vile and profane acts. Each of us has a responsibility to preserve, with dignity and reverence, those sacred things that are given to us of God. Personal testimonies, special spiritual experiences, the name of God, temples and chapels, sacrament meetings, and ordinances such as the sacrament are just some of the things that we need to protect us from the world's degrading encroachments.

One bishop, recognizing the importance of worthiness when using the holy priesthood, called an inactive father in to meet with him. The bishop told him that he would not be able to baptize his daughter unless he became worthy to do so. This man and his wife then spent over an hour with the bishop, trying to understand what the father's worthiness had to do with baptizing their daughter. They said that no one had complained when he had baptized their other children. At the end of the hour, the bishop prayed with the parents and asked them to ponder and pray about what they had discussed. The family followed the bishop's counsel and began bringing their entire family to church. Not only was the father able to baptize his daughter, but also one of his sons, who was totally inactive at the time, ended up becoming involved in the Church and serving a full-time mission. The opportunity to participate in a priesthood ordinance is a sacred thing and should be approached seriously.

One young deacon learned this lesson the hard way. One Sunday, after helping to pass the sacrament, he was sitting on the front bench talking and playing around with his friend. As a shadow fell upon him, he looked up to see his father standing in front of him. His father reached over and grabbed the boy's ear with one hand and his friend's ear with the other. He then proceeded to twist and lift the two boys quickly to their feet. The father then quietly marched the two boys down the aisle and out the back door of the chapel. He taught them a simple but profound lesson when he said, "When you use the priesthood to do something for the Lord, do it right!" These young men never forgot this advice and since then have always taken their participation in priesthood ordinances seriously.

Reverence towards sacred things invites revelation into our lives. Elder Boyd K. Packer discussed the link between reverence and revelation in this way: "When we return for Sunday meetings, the music, dress, and conduct should be appropriate for worship. Foyers are built into our chapels to allow for the greeting and chatter that are typical of people who love one another. However, when we step into the chapel, we *must!*— each of us *must*—watch ourselves lest we be guilty of intruding when someone is struggling to feel delicate spiritual communications. . . . Leaders should teach that reverence invites revelation." ("Reverence Invites Revelation," *Ensign,* November 1991, p. 22.)

The Lord said, "Trifle not with sacred things" (D&C 6:12). "Remember that that which cometh from above is sacred, and must be spoken with care, and by constraint of the Spirit" (D&C 63:64). Because Samuel desired to do the Lord's will and approached his spiritual duties with humility and reverence, he received and recognized the promptings of the Spirit. As we approach the sacred things in our lives with these same attitudes, we will also receive the spiritual guidance we desire and need. Tremendous spiritual blessings will come into our lives as we develop the attitude, "Speak, Lord; for thy servant heareth."

28

The Rise and Fall of Saul

1 SAMUEL 9–10, 13, 15

In the April 1978 general conference, President Ezra Taft Benson warned us of the destructive effect that pride can have on our spiritual growth. He declared that "pride is the great stumbling block to Zion" and that "it limits or stops [our] progression." (Ensign, May 1989, pp. 6, 7.)

A direct opposite of pride is humility. To be truly humble is to be free from pride and arrogance with the realization that we can accomplish little of real worth without the help of God and others. As Jesus plainly demonstrated during his mortal ministry, humility is not a companion of weakness; rather, it is accompanied by a quiet strength that comes from being in tune with the Spirit. The following examples of humility were once given by President Kimball at a BYU devotional.

> I saw humility once when she was baptized in a simple white gown—no ornaments nor makeup, no ostentation or show; yet she and her husband were immensely wealthy. No special favors did she ask. She was immersed, though clothing would be clinging, her hair would be stringing, willing to acknowledge her need for the gospel, the Lord, and his people. She had been as one on a raft, floating in mid-ocean

without oars, sails or engines, or like the groping blind man alone in unfrequented places.

I saw humility receive the Aaronic Priesthood, though he was a businessman of much affluence—tall, handsome, successful, prominent. He walked with the deacons—the twelve-year-olds—to pass the sacrament and radiate in his new opportunity, realizing that "not where we serve, but how we serve" is the true test of greatness. . . .

I saw humility singing in the choir. She sang in many great productions, but now in the ward choir, grateful for the opportunity. I heard her sweet testimony after the administration when she was miraculously healed. A new light in her eyes as she gave thanks to her Lord for her recovery. (BYU, January 16, 1963.)

The great blessings received through humility are contrasted with the destructive power of pride throughout the scriptures, but nowhere are they better seen than in the life of Saul. As a youth, Saul had every reason to be proud, but he wasn't. He had many good qualities, was very handsome, and "from his shoulders and upward he was [taller] than any of the people" (1 Samuel 9:2). Yet when Samuel told him that he had been chosen to lead Israel, Saul humbly replied, "Am not I a Benjamite, of the smallest of the tribes of Israel? and my family the least of all the families of the tribe of Benjamin? wherefore then speakest thou so to me?" (1 Samuel 9:21.)

Because of Saul's humility and righteousness, the Lord told the prophet Samuel to take a vial of oil and anoint Saul to be the first king over Israel. Following his anointing, God gave Saul a "new heart" and the Spirit came upon him. Although priests were also anointed, from this point in the Old Testament usually only the king is referred to as the anointed of the Lord. Anointing signified that the Lord had chosen the person for a particular task and would bestow on that person the traits necessary to successfully perform the calling.

Although God had chosen Saul to lead Israel, Saul had not as yet been presented to or accepted by the people. In order to do this, Samuel called the people together. Through Samuel, the Lord had warned the people what would happen if they chose to be ruled by kings, but the people had ignored the counsel of the Lord and had said, "Nay; but we will have a king over us; that we also may be like all the nations." (1 Samuel 8:19–20.) Things haven't changed much through the years. Many people today still reject God's counsel in order to conform to those around them and to be accepted by others.

Samuel warned the people one last time before presenting Saul to them as their king:

> Thus saith the Lord God of Israel, I brought up Israel out of Egypt, and delivered you out of the hand of the Egyptians, and out of the hand of all kingdoms, and of them that oppressed you:
>
> And ye have this day rejected your God, who himself saved you out of all your adversities and your tribulations; and ye have said unto him, Nay, but set a king over us. Now therefore present yourselves before the Lord by your tribes, and by your thousands. (1 Samuel 10:18–19.)

Samuel then presented Saul to the people by saying, "See ye him whom the Lord hath chosen, that there is none like him among all the people?" (1 Samuel 10:24.) The hearts of many were touched by the Spirit of God, but others refused to accept him as their king.

When an Ammonite army attacked the Israelites, Saul gathered together those who believed in him and soundly defeated the Ammonites. Following this victory, the people wanted to put to death those Israelites who had rejected Saul as their king, but Saul demonstrated the goodness of his heart by saying, "There shall not a man be put to death this day: for to day the Lord hath wrought salvation in Israel" (1 Samuel 11:13). Because of this victory, all of the people followed Saul to Gilgal, where they accepted him as their king and performed sacrifices to the Lord.

The Lord has warned us that most people set their hearts upon "the things of this world, and aspire to the honors of men." Because of this, he said, almost all men, as soon as they get a little authority, "begin to exercise unrighteous dominion." (See D&C 121:35, 39.) In spite of Saul's great humility and righteousness at the time of his call, he soon became important in his own sight and started to go contrary to God's wishes.

After Saul had served as king for two years, Israel was faced by a Philistine army of thirty thousand chariots, six thousand horsemen, and soldiers that were "as the sand which is on the sea shore in multitude" (1 Samuel 13:5). When the Israelites saw the size of the opposing army they were afraid, and many of them began to leave Saul's army. Samuel had promised to make offerings to God before Israel went to battle, and he had directed Saul to await his arrival and instructions. When the appointed day arrived, Saul saw that his army was scattering and did not wait for Samuel; instead, he offered a burnt offering himself.

This was a serious sin for two reasons. First of all, Saul did not have the authority necessary to offer a sacrifice in behalf of the people. Referring to this unauthorized act, Elder James E. Talmage said, "Growing impatient at Samuel's delay, Saul prepared the burnt offering himself, forgetting that though he occupied the throne, wore the crown, and bore the scepter, these insignia of kingly power gave him no right to officiate even as a deacon in the Priesthood of God" (*The Articles of Faith* [Salt Lake City: Deseret Press, 1899], 185).

Saul's other sin was disobedience to the prophet. Samuel had directed Saul to await his arrival and instructions, but Saul actually thought he could strengthen Israel's chances against the Philistines by disregarding the instructions of the Lord's prophet.

Shortly after making the offering, Saul learned that Samuel was coming and went out to greet him. When Samuel asked what he had done, Saul gave a classic answer, an answer that demonstrated that he felt little remorse or repentance for his actions. He told how his army had been getting smaller each day and how the Philistine army had been growing in numbers. He said that he had been afraid that the Philistines would attack him before Samuel made supplication to the Lord, so he had "forced [himself] therefore, and offered a burnt offering" (1 Samuel 13:12).

Saul foolishly violated a fundamental principle of the gospel: no one can receive God's help by disobeying the counsel of his representatives. Saul had wrongly felt that he had the right to override the prophet's instructions and the authority to perform priesthood ordinances, even though he did not hold the priesthood. Because of his pride, arrogance, and disobedience, Saul was told that the kingdom would be given to another.

If Saul felt any repentance at all it soon dissipated, and it wasn't long until he disobeyed the Lord again. The Amalekites were longstanding Israelite enemies, and their destruction had been foretold for hundreds of years. Saul was commanded to smite and destroy the Amalekites and all that they had. But Saul and his people spared "the best of the sheep, and of the oxen, and of the fatlings, and the lambs, and all that was good . . . : but every thing that was vile and refuse, that they destroyed utterly" (1 Samuel 15:9). They gave to the Lord, through destruction, only what was despised and weak and kept the best for themselves. Because the people, including Saul, refused to listen to the Lord, they lost his help and guidance.

Following the victory, Saul went to Carmel and set up a monument in his own honor. By this time Saul's humility had been completely replaced by pride, arrogance, and the desire for earthly fame and wealth.

When Samuel finally tracked him down, Saul lied to this great prophet and said, "Blessed be thou of the Lord: I have performed the commandment of the Lord." Samuel rejected this lie by saying, "What meaneth then this bleating of the sheep in mine ears, and the lowing of the oxen which I hear?" (1 Samuel 15:13–14.)

Saul immediately shifted the blame to the people and said that they had saved the best of the sheep and oxen for a sacrifice to the Lord. Samuel did not accept this explanation but instead accused Saul of keeping the sheep and oxen for himself. Samuel told him that he had been little in his own sight when he had been anointed as king, but now he refused to obey the voice of the Lord.

Saul still would not admit to his own guilt but once again claimed that he had obeyed the Lord and that the animals had been saved for a sacrifice to the Lord. Samuel then taught Saul a lesson that is still applicable today. He said, "Hath the Lord as great delight in burnt offerings and sacrifices as in obeying the voice of the Lord? Behold, to obey is better than sacrifice." (1 Samuel 15:22.)

The ordinance of sacrifice, which looked forward to the atonement of the Savior, was later replaced by the sacrament ordinance. It is important to go to church and partake of the sacrament, but without obedience to the gospel, the ordinance is meaningless and can even be detrimental; "for whoso eateth and drinketh [the sacramental emblems] unworthily eateth and drinketh damnation to his soul" (3 Nephi 18:29).

The blessings of every ordinance are based on obedience to the gospel of Jesus Christ. How foolish Saul was to think that he and the people could receive the Spirit of God through ordinances only!

After this chastisement, Saul finally admitted that he had sinned, but still he tried to place the blame on the people: "I feared the people, and obeyed their voice." Showing his total misunderstanding of the connection between obedience and blessings, he said, "I have sinned: yet honour me now, I pray thee, before the elders of my people, and before Israel, and turn again with me, that I may worship the Lord thy God." Saul seemed more concerned about avoiding an open break with the prophet, which would undermine his authority as king, than he did with being forgiven and worshiping the Lord. (1 Samuel 15:24, 30.)

Saul did begin to outwardly worship the Lord, but he never again lived righteously enough to have the Spirit of the Lord with him. He became jealous of David and sought his life. When some priests showed kindness to David, Saul had them killed. When he became afraid and troubled, he sought revelation from the witch of En-dor. Even though Saul continued to be king, the Lord began to prepare David to take over the throne.

Saul's story is not an unusual one. Many talented men and women have allowed themselves to be filled with pride and have thereby lost the joy and guiding influence of the Spirit of God. The importance of overcoming pride and maintaining humility was taught by President Wilford Woodruff:

> If the President of the Church or either of his counselors or of the apostles or any other man feels in his heart that God cannot do without him, and that he is especially important in order to carry on the work of the Lord, he stands upon slippery ground. I heard Joseph Smith say that Oliver Cowdery, who was the second apostle in this Church, said to him, "If I leave this Church it will fall."

Said Joseph, "Oliver, you try it." Oliver tried it. He fell; but the kingdom of God did not. I have been acquainted with other apostles in my day and time who felt that the Lord could not do without them; but the Lord got along with his work without them. (*Discourses of Wilford Woodruff,* comp. G. Homer Durham [Salt Lake City: Bookcraft, 1946], p. 123.)

Each of us can do an important work in building the kingdom of God, but none of us is indispensable. And we can do little without the Lord's help. We can teach the gospel in a classroom, but only the Spirit can carry the word into the hearts of the students. We can perform sacred ordinances as holders of the priesthood, but only God can bring to pass the promised covenants. We can strive to help our children grow spiritually and come to love the Lord, but without the help of the Spirit and others our efforts will not be successful. Only as we come to realize our total dependency upon the Lord and turn to him for guidance and direction will we successfully fill our Church and family callings.

29

Is There Not a Cause?

1 SAMUEL 16–17

One day an LDS institute teacher became upset when he heard two girls whispering during the opening prayer. These same two girls whispered throughout the class, seemingly oblivious to the dirty looks the teacher directed their way. The instructor was tempted to confront the girls and tell them to leave if they had such pressing information to discuss, but something kept him from unleashing his negative feelings during class.

When the class was over, the two girls approached the teacher, one of them apologized for not having talked with him before class. She explained that her friend was deaf and could read lips, but because the teacher had discussed several things while writing on the board, she had not been able to understand what he was saying. Because of this, the deaf girl's friend had been sharing the teacher's message with her. The teacher later said, "To this day I am thankful that both of us were spared the embarrassment that might have occurred had I given vent to a judgment made without knowing the facts." (Arthur R. Bassett, "Floods, Winds, and the Gates of Hell," *Ensign,* June 1991, p. 8.)

Very often it is easy to jump to some conclusion concerning another's behavior or appearance when we do not have all of the facts. Most of the time, these judgments are inaccurate and lead to decisions and behavior that are detrimental to us and to those being judged.

As the Lord guided Samuel in selecting a replacement for King Saul, he taught us a great lesson concerning judgment. The Lord had indicated that one of the sons of a man named Jesse would be the new king, but it was up to Samuel to identify which son the Lord had chosen. When Samuel saw Eliab, he was so impressed with his size and looks that he was sure he was the Lord's anointed one. However, the Lord told Samuel: "Look not on his countenance, or on the height of his stature; because I have refused him: for the Lord seeth not as man seeth; for man looketh on the outward appearance, but the Lord looketh on the heart" (1 Samuel 16:7).

Because we can only see the outward appearance and actions of others, whereas God sees clearly inner motives and feelings, the only way that we can judge righteously is with the Spirit of the Lord. God explained this to us in the Doctrine and Covenants: "And now, verily, verily, I say unto thee, put your trust in that Spirit which leadeth to do good—yea, to do justly, to walk humbly, to judge righteously; and this is my Spirit" (D&C 11:12).

Samuel listened to the Spirit of God and did not choose Eliab as the next king of Israel. He had seven of Jesse's sons pass before him, and when none of these sons was the Lord's chosen one Samuel asked Jesse if he had any other sons. He was informed that Jesse's youngest son, David, was out in the fields taking care of the sheep. When Samuel's eyes rested on David, the Lord said, "Arise, anoint him: for this is he" (1 Samuel 16:12). Although he had been chosen and anointed by the Lord, only Jesse's family knew at this time that David was going to be the new king.

The Spirit of the Lord had departed from Saul, and his spirit had become deeply troubled. When his servants suggested that beautiful harp music would bring peace to his soul, he sought someone who could play the harp for him when he was especially troubled. One of his servants recommended David, and Saul came to love David greatly. David not only played music for him but also became his armor bearer. David spent part of his time with Saul, and the rest of his time he used to care for his father's sheep.

About this time the Philistines gathered together a great army and prepared to attack Israel. Saul and his army assembled to defend themselves. It was a custom among the Greeks and Philistines to sometimes decide issues of war through chosen champions who represented each army in personal combat. This was a way of determining who the gods wanted to win without going through the bloodshed of a costly battle. The outcome of the contest would determine the winner of the battle, and only one person would die.

The Philistines had such a champion by the name of Goliath. His height was six cubits and a span. A cubit was the distance from the elbow to the tip of the extended middle finger (around 18 inches), and a span was the distance from the thumb to the end of the little finger when the fingers are spread as wide as possible (around 9 inches). Using these measurements, Goliath was approximately nine feet, nine inches tall.

Very few people today reach the height of even seven feet, but it is believed that there were men in Old Testament times that far exceeded this height. The scriptures refer to giants at the time of both Noah and Enoch, and again later when the Israelites entered the promised land. The Israelites referred to these people as Anakims, which in Hebrew means "long-necked" or "tall." These giants were "utterly destroyed," except for those who lived in Gaza, Gath, and Ashdod (see Joshua 11:21–22). Goliath came from the city of Gath. Not only was Goliath over nine and a half feet tall, but he was also covered with armor and had a shield bearer who went before him. He wore a helmet of brass on his head, and his body was covered with a coat of mail that probably weighed over 150 pounds. He had protective pieces of armor (greaves) from his knees to his ankles, his spear was like a weaver's beam, and the spearhead weighed between twelve and twenty-six pounds.

Even though David was Saul's armor bearer, apparently he was permitted to go home from time to time, for he was not at the battlefield when Goliath first offered his challenge. The Philistines had gathered on a mountain on one side of the valley of Elah, and the Israelites were on a mountain on the other side. Goliath went out away from his army and yelled his challenge to the Israelite army, saying, "Choose you a man for you, and let him come down to me. If he be able to fight with me, and to kill me, then will we be your servants: but if I prevail against him, and kill him, then shall ye be our servants, and serve us." He went on to say, "I defy the armies of Israel this day; give me a man, that we may fight together." (1 Samuel 17:8–10.)

Every morning and evening for forty days Goliath went forward and presented his challenge, but the Israelites were greatly afraid and no one was willing to go against him in battle—until David arrived on the scene. Shortly after David arrived at the battlefield, Goliath again stepped forward and mocked Israel. David was amazed that no one trusted in the Lord enough to respond to Goliath's challenge, and he said, "Who is this uncircumcised Philistine [unbeliever], that he should defy the armies of the living God?" When David's older brother Eliab heard David's comment, he put him down, but David responded by saying, "Is there not a cause?" (1 Samuel 17:26, 29.)

David's comment, "Is there not a cause?" suggests that there are times when all of us should stand up and be counted on the side of truth and righteousness. If we saw some high school students beating up a ten-year-old boy, we would feel the need to intercede even if it came to physically defending ourselves and the boy. If a woman was being attacked by someone, and we heard her cries for help, we would be justified in using physical force to help her, because such a cause is a just one. Sometimes God expects us to stand up in other ways for the cause of truth and righteousness and fight such things as pornography, immorality, bigotry, and injustice in our neighborhoods and communities. In David's case, the Philistines were mocking God and his covenants and were striving to take away his people's agency and freedom.

It is evident that Saul had forgotten the Lord's power, which had been demonstrated several times in his own life, for he said to David, "Thou art not able to go against this Philistine to fight with him: for thou art but a youth, and he a man of war" (1 Samuel 17:33). David explained how, with the Lord's help, he had killed a lion and a bear and said, "This uncircumcised Philistine shall be as one of them, seeing he hath defied the armies of the living God" (1 Samuel 17:36).

Saul offered David his armor, but David had never fought with armor before so he took his staff in his hand, chose five smooth stones from the brook, and went out to meet Goliath armed with his shepherd's sling and a deep faith in God.

The slings used in those days were actually very powerful and potent weapons. They were made from a small pouch of leather that could securely hold a stone about the size of a baseball. This pouch was attached to two cords of rope or leather that were about two feet long. Placing a round stone in the pouch and twirling the sling above the head, the slinger could release the stones at a tremendous rate of speed. Some of the better slingers could hurl a stone close to one hundred miles an hour.

Usually the stones were about the size of a baseball and round and smooth in shape. Any variation from perfect round-ness affected the accuracy of the throw. When you envision a stone the size of a baseball hitting Goliath in the forehead at the speed of one hundred miles per hour, it is no wonder that the stone made a deep impression on his mind.

Slings were commonly used in the ancient Near East, and many armies included trained slingers. The best and most accu-rate slingers, however, were usually shepherds, who had many hours each day in which to practice and who used this skill in both herding and protecting their sheep.

Although David believed in his own skills as a slinger, the true source of his courage was his deep faith and trust in God. The Philistines had made a mockery of God and his covenant people, and David knew the Lord would be with him.

When Goliath saw David coming, he scornfully said, "Am I a dog, that thou comest to me with staves?" and he began to curse him (1 Samuel 17:43). David answered him with some of the most beautiful words ever recorded in the scriptures: "Thou comest to me with a sword, and with a spear, and with a shield: but I come to thee in the name of the Lord of hosts, the God of the armies of Israel, whom thou hast defied. This day will the Lord deliver thee into mine hand . . . , that all the earth may know that there is a God in Israel." (1 Samuel 17:45–46.)

As Goliath drew near, David ran to meet him. He took a stone from his bag, placed it in the sling, whirled the sling around, and smote the Philistine in the forehead. He then cut off Goliath's head with the giant's own sword. When the Philistines saw their champion die, they turned and ran—in spite of the promise they had made to serve Israel if Goliath lost. The Israelites pursued them and killed many of them.

Faith, courage, and trust in the Lord are just some of the important qualities that David demonstrated in these Old Testament chapters. One of the important principles taught by this story is that each of us can approach and overcome serious problems and obstacles in our lives. The following steps discuss the correlation between David overcoming Goliath and each of us overcoming our personal challenges.

1. *Some problems seem almost insurmountable.* Goliath was nine and a half feet tall, and, with his training and armor, the men of Israel felt he was unbeatable. He was just too large to handle. Some of the situations we face seem the same way. We just can't see how we are ever going to overcome them and get on with our lives.

2. *Fear and retreat never solve problems.* The Israelites reacted to Goliath with fear; every time he approached, they retreated further into their own camp. Every morning and evening for forty days they retreated, yet their problem was still there. Most problems do not go away or solve themselves. Trying to avoid our problems or running from them will not help them disappear. In fact, most of the time this kind of behavior just makes our problems worse.

3. *Israel made two serious mistakes.* Israel did not have to send out a champion. They could have rejected Goliath's offer and sent out their army instead. When they allowed their enemies to establish the rules, they gave them a great advantage. Many people today, when faced with an important decision, allow friends, family members, or others to make it instead of deciding for themselves. Each one of us needs to decide what we really want out of life and then work toward these goals. Many imagined or potential problems disappear as we clarify our goals.

The Israelites had also forgotten the power of the Lord. No matter how powerful Goliath might have been, his power was infinitesimal compared to God's power. God has promised that he will help us fulfill our righteous objectives. Nephi explained this principle when he declared, "I know that the Lord giveth no commandments unto the children of men, save he shall prepare a way for them that they may accomplish the thing which he commandeth them" (1 Nephi 3:7). As we strive to live righteously and bless the lives of others, God will help us overcome our obstacles—even if they seem nine and a half feet tall.

4. *It is important to remember who we are.* David remembered that he was a literal son of God and a member of God's covenant people. He realized that as a covenant person he represented God and that God would be with him as he went into battle to defend his people. As we remember that we are of a celestial lineage, we realize that with our Heavenly Father's help we can overcome our problems and, in fact, become gods ourselves. In our quest for eternal life, nothing is more important than the realization that we are literal sons and daughters of God and can become like him.

5. *Some things are worth fighting for.* When David said, "Is there not a cause?" he was suggesting that there are some things that are worth fighting for. Captain Moroni acknowledged this when he said this people should be willing to fight for "God, our religion, and freedom, and our peace, our wives, and our children" (Alma 46:12).

The road to eternal life is filled with obstacles and problems that we must overcome in order to receive the promised blessings. It is the very act of overcoming these obstacles that develops the traits that make us more like God. When we are faced with problems and wonder why life has to be so difficult, it is helpful to remember what we are fighting for.

6. *Obedience is a key to overcoming our problems.* The source of David's confidence was his obedience. God has told us that when we live the gospel, demonstrate charity for others, and have virtuous thoughts and desires, our confidence will "wax strong" and we will receive his power (see D&C 121: 41–46). When we live the gospel, we feel confident that God will answer our prayers and bless us with the strength we need. Obedience is a basic ingredient of successful problem-solving.

Part of David's confidence was based on past experiences in which the Lord had interceded in his behalf. He said that he did not want to use Saul's armor because he had not proved it. Talking about tithing, God said, "Prove me now . . . , if I will not open you the windows of heaven, and pour you out a blessing" (Malachi 3:10). As we live the law of tithing and receive the promised blessings, we are prepared for times in our lives when tithing may be more difficult to pay. As we receive the peace and comfort that come from forgiving an offense, we are more confident that God will help us forgive future offenses. As we prove the gospel in our lives, we develop a trust in God that can come in no other way.

7. *We need to ask for the Lord's help to attack our problems.* David didn't hide behind a rock and wait for Goliath to get near—he *ran* to meet him! Most problems will not be solved until we face up to them and form a plan of attack.

Even though David was skilled with a sling, he didn't attempt to attack Goliath alone. He went into battle knowing the Lord was on his side. This same principle applies to us. As we make God our partner, we can receive the strength we so much need and desire.

8. *We can become an inspiration to others.* When Goliath was killed, the Philistines ran. Goliath's failure undermined their own courage and confidence. Just the opposite happened with the Israelites. When David succeeded, their confidence increased and they began to attack the Philistines.

As the Lord helps us overcome obstacles in our lives, others gain confidence that the Lord can and will help them. All of us have been inspired and spiritually regenerated by those who have overcome great obstacles or have learned to cheerfully cope with serious problems in their lives. Our wards and stakes are full of people who, with the Lord's help, are facing the challenges of this world head on. Their problems are making them stronger, not weaker, and they are receiving the peace and happiness that come from fulfilling their eternal destiny and possessing the guidance of the Spirit.

30

Thou Art the Man

2 SAMUEL 11–12

On a hot summer day in Utah, the wind fanned embers from a small campfire into a roaring forest fire that quickly covered the entire mountainside. Before the courageous fire fighters were able to contain the flames, two men were dead, eighteen homes were destroyed, and the beautiful scenery and beneficial assets of the mountain had been devastated. Referring to this fire, Elder Joseph B. Wirthlin warned, "We risk similar damage to our moral integrity when we let our guard down for even one brief moment. The spark of an evil thought can enter our mind that could ignite and destroy the moral fiber of our soul." ("The Straight and Narrow Way," *Ensign,* November 1990, p. 65.)

How sin's destructive forces can start with a thought and grow until they destroy a soul is clearly illustrated in David's relationship with Bath-sheba. Here was a man of great faith whom God had chosen and anointed to be the king over all of Israel, yet because he let his moral and spiritual guard down, he brought great misery and suffering on both himself and his family. As we study David's moral fall, we can identify some important safeguards to help us avoid the misery and heartache that he went through.

1. *It is important to be where we should be.* "At the time when kings go forth to battle," David sent his army off to fight the Ammonites, but he tarried at Jerusalem (2 Samuel 11:1). The

armies usually went off to war in April or May immediately after the grain harvest. In this instance, the holy ark of the covenant was at the battlefield, which is quite damning for David because this symbolized that while the Lord was in the field with the army, David was living a leisurely life at home.

Had David been where he was supposed to be, he may have avoided the sin and heartache that soon became part of his life. In our day, a young man was accidently killed while fooling around with a friend at two o'clock in the morning. Had he been at home in bed, where young men should be at that time in the morning, he would probably still be alive today.

A young girl was injured for life when the car she was in was involved in an accident. She was supposed to be in school, but she was sluffing with a few of her friends. She will be physically handicapped for the rest of her life because she was where she should not have been.

Although these last two examples deal with physical destruction, spiritual destruction starts the same way. There are certain places we should be in at certain times of our lives. When we are somewhere else instead, we lose a portion of God's intended blessings and place ourselves in spiritual danger. For example, a normal young LDS man should be on a mission when he is nineteen and twenty years old; and all of us who can be should be in church each Sabbath day. If we are somewhere else instead because of a lack of dedication, we have already started down a path that leads toward more sin and away from the celestial kingdom.

2. *Temptation needs to be repelled, not embraced.* Anciently, most of the homes in the Middle East were built with flat roofs. On hot summer nights, many people would walk or sit on their roofs and enjoy the cool evening breezes. Because it was much cooler outside than inside, it was also very common for people to sleep on the roofs of their houses.

Evidently David was having trouble getting to sleep, for he "arose from off his bed, and walked upon the roof of the king's house" (2 Samuel 11:2). His palace was probably much higher than most houses, which would make it easy for him to see into the inner courts of nearby homes. As David took his restless walk on the roof, he saw "a woman washing herself; and the woman was very beautiful to look upon."

In spite of how well we live, we are all confronted with temptation. The key to maintaining our spirituality is how we react to temptation when it invades our lives. It looks as though David, when he saw Bath-sheba bathing, did not turn away but continued to look upon her. From his future actions we infer that he allowed lust to enter his heart.

One Church leader told a parable that demonstrates how we should act when we come face to face with temptation. In this parable, a vile man knocked on a family's front door. In spite of the way he was dressed and the vulgar language he was using, the family invited the man into their living room, enjoyed the filthy jokes and stories he told, and made him feel right at home. The next day the man knocked on another family's door. Because they were accustomed to being neighborly, they allowed the man to come into their waiting room. However, this family reacted differently than the first family. As the man started sharing his filth with them, the family did not invite him into their living room but quickly asked him to leave.

Many people respond to evil thoughts in the same way as the first family. When an evil thought enters their mind, some people invite it in, enjoy its company, and savor it as long as possible. Others reject evil thoughts as soon as they enter, by turning away from the stimuli that brought the thought and consciously replacing it with something more inspiring and worthwhile. Apparently, David not only enjoyed lustful thoughts while watching Bath-sheba but also continued to have these thoughts until they led him to act sinfully.

3. *When we allow evil thoughts to linger, they can lead to evil actions.* When David enquired about the woman, he found out that her name was Bath-sheba and that she was the wife of Uriah the Hittite. Uriah was a member of David's royal army guard, and David knew that he was not at home but was where David should have been—at the battlefield. Uriah, whose name meant "My light is the Lord," was a Hittite who had been converted to the Israelite faith.

In spite of the fact that Bath-sheba was married, David sent for her. Sometimes we feel that we can get close to sin without being burned, and maybe David's only intention was to get a closer look at Bath-sheba. Even if David was not planning on being immoral with Bath-sheba, he should have been smarter than to invite her into his home. As soon as he learned that she was married, he should have dismissed his inappropriate thoughts and desires and asked the Lord to help him do so. Part of his problem may revert back to his not being where he should have been. When we aren't doing what we know we should be doing, we find it difficult to pray to the Lord.

4. *Immorality doesn't happen all at once but is usually the result of many previous choices each of which seemed unimportant at the time.* Many young people who would never dream of being immoral start dating at a young age, steady date with one particular person, start parking where they can be alone, begin to neck and pet on a serious level, and eventually completely lose their chastity. Each step was a wrong one, yet Satan led them so carefully and quietly that they never realized they were being misled at all.

Satan uses this same type of approach on adults, including Latter-day Saints. Because most of us have high standards, Satan knows that we will reject the big sins we are faced with, so he cunningly and quietly introduces smaller sins into our lives. He gets us to flirt a little at the office, wear immodest clothing, or view inappropriate videos and television shows. Each of these actions is wrong, but Satan convinces us that they won't really hurt us. Once we are on his path and have left the strait and narrow way of God, Satan continues to lead us until we do things that we would never have thought possible even in our wildest imaginations.

This was the case with David. Immorality entered his life through a series of wrong choices; finally, he sinned seriously against both himself and God. Not being where he should have been and an innocent walk on the roof had led to the abhorrent sin of immorality. But David's downhill slide was not over yet.

5. *Trying to hide our sins instead of confessing and repenting of them usually leads to greater sins.* The scriptures indicate that Bath-sheba was able to respond to David's invitation to visit him because she "was purified from her uncleanness" (2 Samuel 11:4). She had just become ceremonially clean after her seven-day period of monthly impurity due to menstruation. This is an important phrase and was placed in the scriptures to show that Bath-sheba was not pregnant from her husband at the time of her sexual relations with David. When she became pregnant, she knew that David had to be the baby's father.

Both David and Bath-sheba knew that the law required the death penalty for adultery. When Bath-sheba sent word to David that she was pregnant, he immediately tried to cover their sin. David's plan was to have Uriah come home and sleep with his wife; thus the baby would be considered Uriah's, and David's immorality would remain hidden. Throughout this series of events, David doesn't appear to give much thought to the Lord and the fact that he would know everything that David was doing.

Because of Uriah's great devotion to the Lord, and his loyalty to the troops in the field, this plan just didn't work. David had Uriah leave the battlefield and report to him under the pretext of finding out how the battle was going. After Uriah had given his report, David told him to go home and spend the night, but he slept at the door of the king's palace instead. When David asked him why he had not gone home, Uriah replied, "The ark [of the covenant], and Israel, and Judah, abide in tents; and my lord Joab, and the servants of my lord, are encamped in the open fields; shall I then go into mine house, to eat and to drink, and to lie with my wife? as thou livest, and as thy soul liveth, I will not do this thing." (2 Samuel 11:11.) Uriah's devotion to duty sharply contrasted with David's presence at his palace.

Following this failure, David got Uriah drunk in the hope that he would go home to his wife, but he slept with the palace servants instead. David, still totally unrepentant, then took the irrevocable step of planning Uriah's murder in order to hide his sin.

Up to this point, sincere repentance could have brought to David a remission of sins, but this act now put him beyond the great gift of repentance:

> [Murder is a] "sin unto death" . . . , a sin for which there is "no forgiveness." . . . [A murderer] is outside the pale of redeeming grace. . . .
>
> Murderers are forgiven eventually but only in the sense that all sins are forgiven except the sin against the Holy Ghost; they are not forgiven in the sense that celestial salvation is made available to them. . . . After they have paid the full penalty for their crime, they shall go on to a telestial

inheritance. (Bruce R. McConkie, Mormon Doctrine, 2nd ed. [Salt Lake City: Bookcraft, 1966], p. 520.)

Since David had failed in his attempts to make it appear that Uriah was the father, he plotted Uriah's death so he could marry Bath-sheba himself as quickly as possible. David's commander in the field was to set Uriah in the place where the hottest battle was being fought, then quickly withdraw his men so that Uriah would be killed. This plan worked only too well, and David soon became guilty of the sin of murder. As soon as the appointed time for mourning was over, Bath-sheba became David's wife, and both of them thought they had successfully covered their sin. But the thing David had done had greatly displeased the Lord. Not only had he committed adultery and murder but he had also shamelessly abused his royal power, which the Lord had entrusted to him.

Many people today also try to hide their sins by committing sins that are even worse in nature. For example, the heinous sin of abortion has become one prevalent way of attempting to hide the sin of immorality. Instead of facing up to their sins and turning their lives toward God, many misguided and unhappy souls sink deeper into sin, depression, and misery. The earlier we face up to sin, the less difficult it is to repent and the less heartache and misery we bring upon ourselves and others.

6. *No one can sin and get away with it. All sins are known to God, and those not repented of will someday become known to others.* Uriah was dead, the wedding was over, a son had been born to David and Bath-sheba, and it looked as if everything would be just fine—that is, until the prophet Nathan arrived on the scene. God had commanded Nathan to openly confront David about his sins. Nathan did this by telling David the parable of the ewe lamb.

Two men lived in the same city—one was poor and the other one rich. The rich man had a great many flocks and herds, but the poor man only had one little ewe lamb. The poor man's family had nourished this lamb from its birth, and it had grown up with the family until it was considered one of the children. The lamb ate from the poor man's plate, drank from his cup, and slept in his bosom at night.

One day the rich man had a visitor. He didn't want to feed

his visitor from his own flock, so he took the poor man's lamb and killed and dressed it instead.

When David heard this story, his "anger was greatly kindled." He said, "As the Lord liveth, the man that hath done this thing shall surely die; and he shall restore the lamb fourfold, because he did this thing, and because he had no pity." (2 Samuel 12:5–6.)

Then Nathan declared to David: "Thou art the man." In the name of the Lord he described David's great sin before God (2 Samuel 12:7). The Lord had anointed David king over all of Israel and had given him the king's house and many wives. He would have given him numerous other things if only David had asked for them. But instead of being content with the things God had blessed him with, he had despised the commandment of the Lord, killed Uriah the Hittite, and taken Uriah's wife to be his own. Nathan then said that even though David had done these things secretly, all Israel would now know about them.

David was told that he would not be put to death—but his and Bath-sheba's child would die. Nathan explained to him that his enemies would use his sin against the Lord as a reason to sin themselves, and he warned David of the many consequences that would follow his foolish and sinful actions. One of these consequences would be that the sword would never depart from his own house. Contention, immorality, and murder within his own family were some of the fruits of David's actions.

Because David did not repent before murdering Uriah, he "is still paying for his sin" (Joseph Fielding Smith, *Answers to Gospel Questions,* comp. Joseph Fielding Smith, Jr. [Salt Lake City: Deseret Book Co., 1957], 1:74). Once David has paid for his sins in hell, he will go on to a telestial inheritance. President Spencer W. Kimball suggested that

> perhaps the reason murder is an unforgivable sin is that, once having taken a life—whether that life be innocent or reprobate—the life-taker cannot restore it. . . . He might do many other noble things; but a life is gone and the restitution of it in full is impossible. . . .
>
>   . . . To take a life, whether someone else's or one's own, cuts off the victim's experiences of mortality and thus his

opportunity to repent, to keep God's commandments in this earth life. It interferes with his potential of having "glory added upon [his head] for ever and ever." (Abraham 3:26.) (*The Miracle of Forgiveness* [Salt Lake City: Bookcraft, 1969], pp. 195–96.)

If David, as strong as he was, could be led into immorality and even murder, surely each of us needs to be on guard against the numerous temptations Satan places in our lives. In a talk given at Brigham Young University, President Ezra Taft Benson gave the following steps that he said, if followed, will ensure that we never fall into moral transgression.

1. *Decide now to be chaste.* Make that decision now and let it be so firm and with such deep commitment, that it can never be shaken.

2. *Control your thoughts.* No one steps into immorality in an instant. The first seeds of immorality are always sown in the mind. When we allow our thoughts to linger on lewd or immoral things, we have taken the first step on the road to immorality.

3. *Always pray for the power to resist temptation.* Part of our daily prayers should be to ask the Lord for constant strength to resist temptation, especially temptations that involve the law of chastity.

4. *If you are married, avoid flirtations of any kind.* What may appear to be harmless teasing or simply having a little fun with someone of the opposite sex can easily lead to more serious involvement and eventual infidelity.

5. *If you are married, avoid being alone with a member of the opposite sex.* Many of the tragedies of immorality begin when a man and woman are alone in the office, at church, or in a car. One thing leads to another, and very quickly tragedy may result.

6. *For those who are single and dating members of the opposite sex, carefully plan positive and constructive activities so that you are not left to yourselves with nothing to do but share physical affection.* Fill your life so full with positive actions that the negative has no chance to thrive. (See BYU Devotional, October 13, 1987.)

David was a tremendous king but made a tragic mistake from which he could not fully recover. Similarly, success in our

Church callings or in our occupations cannot make up for failure in our personal lives or as parents in our homes. David's life teaches us the importance of enduring to the end. He made great spiritual choices while young and then let exaltation slip through his grasp by slowly but surely sinking deeper and deeper into sin. The "little" things we do and the "small" choices we make are extremely important in our lives, for they determine the course we follow and the eventual reward we receive. When we are faithful in the smaller tasks God wants us to do, we are nearly always faithful in the larger ones. Godlike character is built one decision and one step at a time.

31

We Will Not Serve Thy Gods

DANIEL 1–3, 6

Peer pressure and social acceptance are major forces in our world today. In order to receive acceptance from some person or group or to avoid ridicule or criticism, many people—in their dress, speech, and actions—try to please others rather than themselves and God. A humorous side of this copycat mind-set was described by Jules Feiffer.

> Ever since I was a little kid I didn't want to be me. I wanted to be Billie Widdledon and Billie Widdledon didn't even like me. I walked like "he" walked—I talked like "he" talked—I signed up for the High School "he" signed up for. Which was when Widdledon changed. He began to hang around Herby Vandeman. He mixed me up! I began to walk and talk like Billie Widdledon walking and talking like Herby Vandeman.
> And then it dawned on me that Herby Vandeman walked and talked like Joey Haverlin and Joey Haverlin walked and talked like Corky Sabison. So here I am walking and talking like Billie Widdledon's imitation of Herby Vandeman's version of Joey Haverlin trying to walk and talk like Corky Sabison.
> And who do you think Corky Sabison is always walking

and talking like? Of all people—Dopey Wellington—*that* little pest who walks and talks like me! (Source unknown.)

Although some actions performed to gain acceptance are humorous, often this desire to be accepted has a negative impact on our spiritual growth and our effectiveness as a member of God's kingdom. One teenager described this problem when he wrote: "I hate being embarrassed in front of my friends. I don't dare say anything or do anything that they might make fun of, even if it's the right thing. I won't hug my mom in public. I won't sing in church. I won't answer any questions in class. I'm tired of being such a coward, but I just can't stand humiliation. Is there anything I can do about my problem?"

Every person in all ages has been born with the basic desire to be accepted and loved. Perhaps we could all find the answer to some of our questions by studying the lives of some of the great men and women written about in the scriptures. Four men who had the courage and faith to resist social pressure and stand up for the truth were Daniel, Shadrach, Meshach, and Abed-nego.

They lived about 600 B.C. when, because of gross disobedience to God, the kingdom of Judah had been conquered by Babylonia. It was the custom in those days to remove the skilled and educated from the conquered country in order to weaken its leadership. This made the conquered people easier to govern, and the exiled leaders added great knowledge and strength to the conquering country. Daniel and his friends were part of the first deportation of Israelites to Babylonia, which took place around 600 B.C. There was a second deportation subsequently following the destruction of Jerusalem and the temple.

Daniel and his friends must have been well skilled and educated, for only a select few of the Israelites, including the king's seed and the princes, were taken in the first deportation. The scriptures say that those chosen were "children in whom was no blemish, but well favoured, and skilful in all wisdom, and cunning in knowledge, and understanding science, and such as had ability in them to stand in the king's palace, and whom they might teach the learning and the tongue of the Chaldeans" (Daniel 1:4).

These exiled Jews were to be fed the "king's meat" and were to drink the same wine as the king drank for a period of three years. At the end of this time they would stand before the king, who would decide where and how they would serve the empire.

The Jewish people considered the food and wine from Nebuchadnezzar's table to be contaminated for several reasons. The first portion of his food was offered to idols, and a portion of his wine was poured out on a pagan altar. The animals that were used were ceremonially unclean, for they were neither slaughtered nor prepared according to the Law of Moses. The Jews had been commanded to kill their animals in such a way that much of the blood was drained from them.

Because of these problems, Daniel and his friends decided in their hearts that they would not defile themselves with the king's meat and wine. Because of Daniel's great courage and faith, God brought him into favor and compassion with the "prince of the eunuchs," who was responsible for the education, health, and training of the captured Jews.

When Daniel told the prince that they could not defile themselves with the meat and wine from the king's table, the prince was very concerned. He was afraid that if he allowed Daniel and his three friends to ignore the king's command in this way, they would look less healthy. That could in turn lead to the king beheading the prince of the eunuchs.

Instead of just rebelling and saying that he and his three friends would not partake of the king's food, Daniel suggested an alternative plan. He suggested that for ten days the four of them eat foods (called pulse) made from seeds and grains and drink water instead of the king's wine. At the end of the ten days, the prince could compare the countenances of Daniel and his friends with those who partook of the king's food and then decide whether they could continue on their own diet. At the end of the ten days, Daniel, Shadrach, Meshach, and Abednego looked "fairer and fatter in flesh than all the children which did eat the portion of the king's meat" (Daniel 1:15). Therefore, the prince allowed them to continue on their menu of pulse and water.

Because of their faithfulness, God gave them knowledge, skill, and wisdom. Daniel received an understanding of visions and dreams. At the end of the three years, the king found them ten times more knowledgeable and wise than all of the magicians and astrologers in his realm. Because of this, and because of dreams that Daniel interpreted, they received high positions of authority in the Babylonian empire.

However, this was just the beginning of their test of faith

and obedience. Each one of them would still receive tremendous pressure to lower their values in order to save their lives.

Daniel's three companions were tested first. King Nebuchadnezzar made an image of gold that was ninety feet high and nine feet wide. He then summoned all of his leaders for the dedication of the image. A herald announced that every person, when the signal was given, should fall down and worship the image. He warned that anyone who did not follow his instructions would immediately be thrown into a blazing furnace.

When some jealous Babylonians told the king that Shadrach, Meshach, and Abed-nego refused to worship the golden idol, he became furious. When the three Jews had been brought to Nebuchadnezzar, he asked them if it was true that they refused to serve his gods and worship the image of gold. He warned them that if they continued to refuse, he would have them burned to death.

Shadrach, Meshach, and Abed-nego answered the king: "If it be so, our God whom we serve is able to deliver us from the burning fiery furnace, and he will deliver us out of thine hand, O king. But if not, be it known unto thee, O king, that we will not serve thy gods, nor worship the golden image which thou hast set up." (Daniel 3:17–18.)

This answer so enraged Nebuchadnezzar that he had the furnace heated seven times hotter than usual. He then had the mightiest men in his army bind Shadrach, Meshach, and Abed-nego and cast them into the burning furnace. The furnace was so hot that the flames killed the men who threw them into it.

As Nebuchadnezzar looked into the furnace, he was astonished to see four men walking in the midst of the fire, "the form of the fourth [being] like the Son of God." He approached the mouth of the furnace and told the three Jews to come forth from the midst of the fire.

The king and all of his leaders were amazed to see that the fire had done no damage of any kind to Shadrach, Meshach, and Abed-nego. It had not so much as singed their hair, and the smell of the fire had not even passed onto them or their clothes. The king was so impressed with the power of their God that he made an official decree. He stated that anyone who said anything against their God should be cut into pieces and their houses made into a dunghill, because "there is no other God that can deliver after this sort" (Daniel 3:29). The king then promoted these three faithful and courageous Jews in the province of Babylon.

Years later, Daniel found himself in a similar situation. Darius the Mede had become the ruler over the Babylonian empire and had chosen three presidents to help him administer the kingdom. He had made Daniel the leader of these three presidents, but, because of Daniel's excellent spirit, the king preferred him over the other leaders and was planning on placing him in charge of the whole empire.

The other presidents and princes, being jealous of Daniel, sought to find something against him that they could use to discredit him. However, Daniel was so faithful to his calling and honest in his administration that they could find nothing against him. They decided that their only chance of alienating him from the king was through his obedience to his God, so they developed a plan that they felt could not fail. The plan was based on Daniel's faithfulness and obedience, and they were determined to use these very traits to destroy him.

The jealous leaders met with the king and encouraged him to sign a decree that proclaimed that "whosoever shall ask a petition of any God or man for thirty days, save of thee, O king, he shall be cast into the den of lions" (Daniel 6:7). They knew that Daniel prayed three times a day to his God and that he would continue to do so.

Even though Daniel knew of the decree, he knelt facing toward Jerusalem and offered his prayer to God just as he had done three times each day in the past. When Daniel knelt facing toward Jerusalem, he was following the counsel Solomon gave in the temple's dedicatory prayer: "Pray unto the Lord toward the city which thou hast chosen, and toward the house that I have built for thy name" (1 Kings 8:44). In the dedicatory prayer for the Salt Lake Temple, President Wilford Woodruff said:

Heavenly Father, when thy people shall not have the opportunity of entering this holy house to offer their supplications unto thee, and they are oppressed and in trouble, surrounded by difficulties or assailed by temptation, and *shall turn their faces towards this thy holy house* and ask thee for deliverance, for help, for thy power to be extended in their behalf, we beseech thee to look down from thy holy habitation in mercy and tender compassion upon them, and listen to their cries. (In James E. Talmage, *The House of the Lord* [Salt Lake City: Deseret Book Co., 1968], p. 142; emphasis added.)

When Daniel was brought before the king, the king realized he had been fooled into making a foolish law and was "sore displeased with himself" (Daniel 6:14). The king set his heart on delivering Daniel, laboring until the going down of the sun to find a way to do this. When he tried to revoke the law and release Daniel, the jealous presidents and princes reminded him that, according to the law of the Medes and Persians, once the king had signed a decree it could not be altered or changed in any way.

The king, who seemed to sincerely like and respect Daniel, said to him, "Thy God whom thou servest continually, he will deliver thee" (Daniel 6:16). Daniel was then placed in a den of lions and the mouth of the den sealed with a stone. The king spent the night fasting for Daniel and refused to sleep or listen to music.

Early the next morning the king hastened to the lions' den and cried out, "O Daniel, servant of the living God, is thy God, whom thou servest continually, able to deliver thee from the lions?" (Daniel 6:20.)

The king's heart was filled with joy when Daniel answered, "My God hath sent his angel, and hath shut the lions' mouths, that they have not hurt me." The king commanded that Daniel be taken out of the den, and "no manner of hurt was found upon him, because he believed in his God." It soon becomes clear that the lions were ravenously hungry, yet this was no obstacle to the Lord's rewarding Daniel's faith by saving his life. (Daniel 6:22–24.)

The king now commanded that those men who had accused Daniel, and the men's families, be cast into the den of lions. Before their bodies even reached the den floor, the lions overpowered them and crushed all their bones. The killing of the families was a Persian custom, because out of these families might come insurrection in the future.

The king then signed a decree proclaiming "that in every dominion of my kingdom men tremble and fear before the God of Daniel: for he is the living God. . . . He delivereth and rescueth, and he worketh signs and wonders in heaven and in earth." (Daniel 6:26–27.) Because of his great faith in the living God, Daniel prospered in the reign of Darius and in the reign of Cyrus the Persian. As a matter of fact, Daniel successfully served five different kings without compromising his standards or wavering in his obedience to God.

Elder Charles Didier suggested that one of our real purposes in life is to become a friend of the Savior, "and not only understand his mission but also support it and then qualify to be called his friend." He went on to say, "Are we strong enough to refuse to be a friend of the world and its representatives? Are we strong enough to accept friendship with Christ?" ("Friend or Foe," *Ensign,* November 1983, p. 24.)

Daniel must have faced almost daily challenges to his way of life, which is no different from life for us today. We maintain our friendship with Christ by maintaining our Christlike standards and defending them when needed. A girl named Jenny is one example of how a simple decision to do right can have a positive effect on those around us.

> Jenny went to the movies with friends she'd long wanted to impress. It was fun until the movie was well under way, and then there flashed across the screen some scenes inappropriate for public sharing. She winced and felt sick inside, but she wanted to keep in the good graces of the group. What to do? Besides, she needed a ride home. Finally, she excused herself and determined to wait in the lobby until the show was over. Soon her boyfriend went to find her. He admitted he'd been embarrassed, too. Together they waited for the rest of the group. One by one the others came out, curious and concerned. Because one girl dared to take a stand on her own, others had the courage to follow. (Elaine A. Cannon, "Voices," *New Era,* July 1980, p. 15.)

Peer pressure exerts a powerful influence on those who do not have firm testimonies of the gospel. A recent study suggested that over seventy percent of the major sins committed by teenagers were committed because of peer pressure. Darius the king mentioned twice that Daniel served his God continually. As we make a daily habit of prayer, scripture study, and obedience to the Lord, our own faith and testimonies will grow, and we will receive the strength to put God first in our lives. Not only will this bring great joy and peace into our own lives but also, just as it did with Daniel and Jenny, it will have a positive effect on those we associate with.

32

Jonah
Struggles with His Call

JONAH 1–4

Jonah's story is an unusual one. Like other Old Testament prophets, Jonah was called to cry repentance to a wicked people. Unlike these other prophets, however, Jonah did not want to accept his calling and attempted to avoid his God-given assignment. As the story develops, it appears that he did not reject his call out of fear but rather because he did not want to give an enemy nation a chance to accept the gospel and be forgiven. The story of Jonah carries an important message about (1) the love that God has for all of his children, and (2) our responsibility to share the gospel with friends and enemies alike.

Jonah lived during the reign of Jeroboam II, which would have been around 788 B.C. The Lord called him to preach the gospel to Nineveh and to warn its inhabitants that they would be destroyed unless they repented. Nineveh, which was five hundred miles from where Jonah lived, was first built by Nimrod and was traditionally known as the "great city." About 700 B.C., it became the Assyrian capital, which it remained until its fall in 612. The walls of the city were about eight miles in circumference and one hundred feet high, and were wide enough at the top to permit three chariots to be driven abreast. Greater

Nineveh, which included a complex of cities, covered an area of some sixty miles in circumference.

The Lord said that the people's wickedness had come up before him, which is not surprising, since the Assyrians had been terrorizing the Middle East for almost a hundred years. It is helpful to understand what these people were like in order to better comprehend Jonah's feelings and the great miracle that took place when the Ninevites responded to Jonah's message.

Their cold-blooded cruelty and savagery had struck fear into the hearts of all those who had come in contact with them. Jonah lived when Nineveh was at the height of her violence and power. One ruler's stone carvings boasted of the prolonged torturing of captives, blinding children before the eyes of their parents, skinning men alive, roasting men in kilns, and burying men alive. One king cut off the hands of all those whom he captured and also performed other atrocities so evil and revolting that it is not appropriate to list or discuss them.

It must have seemed preposterous to Jonah that God wanted the gospel preached to the people in this wicked and cruel city—a people Jonah had come to hate and fear. After sorting through his feelings, Jonah decided to reject the call and headed in the opposite direction from Nineveh. He later told the Lord that he had tried to avoid his call because he knew the Lord was a gracious and merciful God who would forgive the people of Nineveh if they repented (see Jonah 4:1–2). Referring to Jonah's strong feelings against the people of Nineveh, Sidney Sperry wrote:

> It was no surprise to the prophet to be called, for he had probably carried out many missions for the Lord in Israel before. His surprise lay not in the *fact* of the call but in the *kind* of call, and rebellion arose in his heart. . . .
>
> Jonah was torn between his loyalty to God and the whip of his emotions. The latter were at a fever pitch and in the end determined his actions. Because he couldn't face the mission call, he determined to flee the country and get away from the unpleasant responsibility. He did not intend to lay down his prophetic office; he merely wanted to absent himself without leave for a time until an unpleasant situation adjusted itself. (*The Voice of Israel's*

Prophets [Salt Lake City: Deseret Book Co., 1952], pp. 328–29.)

Once Jonah decided to flee from the Lord's presence, he went down to the seaport Jappa and boarded a ship going to Tarshish. Many scholars believe that Tarshish is the same place as Tartessus in Spain, which was a considerable distance in the opposite direction from Nineveh.

Although Jonah thought he could avoid his divinely appointed task, the Lord had other plans. He sent a mighty tempest that placed the ship Jonah was on in great jeopardy. The sailors were afraid and called upon their gods to save them. They even threw overboard everything they did not need, in order to lighten the ship. Jonah was oblivious to all of this, as he had gone down into the ship and had fallen into a deep sleep. When the storm did not abate, the shipmaster woke up Jonah and asked him to call upon his God so that their lives might be saved.

The sailors decided that God was angry at someone on the ship, so they cast lots to see who was causing the evil that had befallen them. This was a custom widely practiced in the ancient Near East. Although the precise method is unclear, it appears that sticks or marked pebbles were usually drawn from a container in which they had been cast. This custom was based on the belief that God would show his will through this process. In this case, God did reveal his will, for the lot fell upon Jonah. When Jonah explained that he was a Hebrew and was running away from God of heaven, who had made the sea and dry land, the men's hearts were filled with fear, and they asked what they should do so that Jonah's God would calm the sea. Jonah told them to cast him overboard, but they were concerned for his welfare and began to row strenuously in an effort to bring the ship to dry land. Their reluctance to throw Jonah into the sea stands in sharp contrast to Jonah's lack of concern for the people of Nineveh.

When they realized they would all die if Jonah was not thrown overboard, they prayed that his life would not be held against them and cast him into the raging sea. The sea immediately became calm, and the sailors, recognizing the power of Israel's God, offered a sacrifice and made vows to the Lord.

Ancient pagans believed in the existence and power of many gods. Although there is no evidence that the sailors renounced their previous gods, at least they acknowledged the power of Jonah's God and worshiped him.

The scripture says that the "Lord had prepared a great fish to swallow up Jonah" (Jonah 1:17). This emphasizes that the Lord's power was involved and that the miracle cannot be reasoned away as something that could normally take place. Many Bible scholars have received this account of Jonah with doubt and ridicule. Others have tried to explain away God's power by sharing stories of seamen who have been swallowed by whales and were found alive hours or days later. Joseph Fielding Smith gave his reason for believing in the story of Jonah:

> Are we to reject it as being an impossibility and say that the Lord could not prepare a fish, or whale, to swallow Jonah? . . . Surely the Lord sits in the heavens and laughs at the wisdom of the scoffer, and then on a sudden answers his folly by a repetition of the miracle in dispute, or by the presentation of one still greater. . . .
>
> I believe . . . the story of Jonah. My chief reason for so believing is not in the fact that it is recorded in the Bible, or that the incident has been duplicated in our day, but in the fact that *Jesus Christ, our Lord, believed it.* The Jews sought him for a sign of his divinity. He gave them one, but not what they expected. The scoffers of his day, notwithstanding his mighty works, were incapable, because of sin, of believing.
>
> "He answered and said unto them, An evil and adulterous generation seeketh after a sign; and there shall no sign be given to it, but the sign of the Prophet Jonas: for as Jonas was three days and three nights in the whale's belly; so shall the Son of man be three days and three nights in the heart of the earth." (*Doctrines of Salvation,* comp. Bruce R. McConkie [Salt Lake City: Bookcraft, 1955], 2:314–15.)

Both the Hebrew word *taneen* and the Greek word *katos* do not specify a whale but describe any sea creature of immense size. Sharks are common to the Mediterranean and have throats large enough to swallow a man. The great miracle, however, is not in being swallowed by a large fish, but the fact that Jonah lived for three days inside the fish without the digestive acids destroying his body. This was only accomplished through God's great knowledge and power.

Once Jonah found himself in the belly of the fish, he decided that he could go to Nineveh if that was what the Lord really wanted. He began to praise the Lord for his deliverance and promised that he would keep the vows that he had made. The Lord then spoke to the fish, and it vomited out Jonah upon dry land.

When the Lord asked Jonah the second time to go to Nineveh, it is not very surprising that he responded to the call. After traveling a day's journey into the city, he warned the people that in forty days Nineveh would be overthrown. To his astonishment, the people of the city believed him, proclaimed a fast, and put on sackcloth. Even the king covered himself with sackcloth and sat in ashes to show his repentant and willing spirit.

The king published a decree asking all of the people of Nineveh to go without food and drink, dress in sackcloth, and cry mightily unto God. He said, "Who can tell, if we will repent, and turn unto God, but [that] he will turn away from us his fierce anger, that we perish not?" (JST, Jonah 3:9.) When God saw that they indeed turned from their evil way and repented, he "turned away the evil that he had said he would bring upon them" (JST, Jonah 3:10).

In spite of his success as a missionary, Jonah's bitter feelings against the Assyrians did not change. As a matter of fact, when God said that he would not destroy them, Jonah's hatred and resentment seemed to deepen, and he became exceedingly angry. He told God that this was the very reason why he hadn't wanted to preach to the people—he had known that God would forgive them if they repented. He was angry that God would have compassion on an enemy of Israel and wanted God's goodness to be shown only to Israelites, not to Gentiles. A few days before, Jonah had rejoiced in his deliverance from death, but now he wanted to die rather than watch his enemies be forgiven and blessed by the Lord.

Jonah left the city and found a place to sit where he could watch what happened to Nineveh. Apparently he still hoped that Nineveh would be destroyed. The sun was extremely hot, so he built himself a shelter that afforded him a limited amount of shade. In an effort to teach Jonah that he loved all of his children, God caused a large plant to grow next to Jonah. The plant gave him much-needed protection from the sun, and he was very grateful for the plant. God then prepared a worm that smote the plant and caused it to wither, and Jonah felt distress and anger that God would allow the plant to die.

God then said to Jonah, "Thou hast had pity on the gourd, for the which thou hast not laboured, neither madest it grow; which came up in a night, and perished in a night: and should not I spare Nineveh, that great city, wherein are more than six-score thousand persons that cannot discern between their right hand and their left hand; and also much cattle?" (Jonah 4:10–11.) By means of this simple plant the Lord taught Jonah that people are much more important than plants and that he loves all of his children.

This unconditional love that God feels for each of us is the kind of love that we should develop and nurture in our own lives. The Greek language, from which the New Testament was taken, has three separate words for love: They are *eros, philos,* and *agape.*

Eros is the love of something above ourselves, the love of an adorable object or quality. This type of love is implied when a person speaks of falling in love with love. The excitement associated with dating falls into this category. Eros was the god of love in Greek mythology—the same individual the Romans called Cupid. "Erotic" is the sexual aspect of this love.

Philos is the type of love associated with friendship. From it come such words as *philadelphia* (brotherly love), *philanthropy* (love of man), and *philosophy* (love of wisdom). This love is usually conditional, which means that circumstances determine whether we feel love or friendship for a certain person. If this person does things that we agree with or if our association with him is pleasant, we remain friends. However, if conditions change and conflict enters our relationship, our friendship may come to an end.

Agape is love for those who have done nothing to merit love. It is a love for the undeserving. *Agape* is the word used in the Greek New Testament text in passages in which Christ speaks of love. Agape is the kind of love that God and Jesus have for each of us. It is referred to as charity in the scriptures. All of us have been commanded to develop this love. It is the kind of love that Jonah was lacking for the people of Nineveh.

Jonah's reluctance to accept his call stemmed from his lack of charity for the people and from a deficiency of trust in God. Even though the city was converted, Jonah did not benefit much, because little spiritual growth or true joy comes from reluctant service.

Elder Jack H. Goaslind illustrated the importance of worshiping and serving God with full purpose of heart:

> Several years ago I heard about a good brother who described his attitude as President David O. McKay gave the concluding talk of general conference. It was a sultry afternoon, and this was the fifth session he had attended. He was sitting in the balcony, and his mind had a serious wandering problem. He noticed a man sitting in the middle section who had fallen asleep with his head tilted back and his mouth open. It occurred to him that if he were in the roof of the Tabernacle, he could drop a spit wad through one of the vent holes right into the mouth of that sleeping man. What a glorious thought! Following the meeting, he overheard two men talking about their feelings during President McKay's talk. They were visibly moved by what they had heard. He thought to himself, These two brethren were having a marvelous spiritual experience, and what was I doing? Thinking about dropping spit wads from the ceiling! ("Yagottawanna," *Ensign,* May 1991, p. 46.)

It was just as hot and uncomfortable for those two men as it was for the man in the balcony, yet they got something out of the meeting because they put their hearts into it. Many times we may initially disagree with some counsel or call that is given to us from our Church leaders. If we will trust in their judgment and serve with our hearts as well as our minds and bodies, we will benefit from our service.

One stake presidency became concerned about what was taking place in their fast and testimony meetings. They taught their bishops what pure testimony is and emphasized the power that can come from it. They asked the bishops to teach their people that home evening, not sacrament meeting, is the place to teach children how to bear their testimonies. Miracles began to take place in fast and testimony meetings in the stake. Children began testifying that they knew that Jesus and Heavenly Father loved them and answered their prayers. A great spirit began to accompany sacrament meetings.

The stake president received a letter from a mother who had at first been resentful of the changes the stake president wanted made. A part of her letter reads:

I have to be honest with you. When I learned of your request to teach children how to bear their testimonies at home I was angry with you. I have enjoyed watching my daughter, since she could walk, go to the front with her older brother to bear her testimony. I always thought it was cute watching Jeff telling her what to say. . . .

We trusted you and so we decided to obey your counsel. I want you to know what a wonderful spirit this has brought into our home. Once a month we have a family testimony meeting where our children stand and bear their testimonies at home. We have felt the spirit of our Savior as our children, through our example and teachings, have stood to bear their testimonies of the Savior, the Church, and our Father in Heaven.

It is our favorite evening of the month. We always have a lot of tissue on hand, as it is a tearful meeting, especially for me. Last month our oldest son, now 13, asked an interesting question at the conclusion of our family testimony meeting.

"Dad, what is that strange feeling inside of me? It feels like my heart is on fire."

President, what a joy it is to know that our child has felt the Holy Ghost, and in our home!

We are so blessed. I believe I understand the principle you were trying to teach. Fast and testimony meeting is not a show; it was never designed to be cute. It is a time of strengthening, a time of closeness. How much our family has strayed, how much we have lost in asking our children to be cute in these sacred meetings.

This past fast and testimony meeting, our five-year-old

girl walked to the front all alone. She stood at the micro-phone and said: "My Savior, whose name is Jesus, loves me . . . I love Jesus and He makes me feel good."

She closed and sat down. It was the most incredible tes-timony, and it came from her mouth because of our family home evenings. Thank you, president. Thank you. (Harry F. Schubert, Jr., "Miracles beginning to happen in this stake," *Church News,* November 30, 1991.)

Even though this family initially disagreed with their lead-ers, unlike Jonah they trusted their stake president enough to fulfill the assignment they had been given. Because of their willingness to wholeheartedly obey, they received precious blessings from the Lord.

Effective Church service is simple. President McKay said: "Love the work, do your best, then leave the conversion to the workings of the Spirit of the Lord." He then promised, "When you have done your duty, the peace and satisfaction that come will more than compensate for any rebuff, resentment, or oppo-sition, that might be manifest." When a young home teacher asked if they needed to continue to go back to a home where both the mother and father used tobacco and were planning on continuing to do so, President McKay said, "Yes; go back again and again, you do your duty, and leave the rest to the Lord." (*Gospel Ideals* [Salt Lake City: The Improvement Era, 1957], p. 174.)

As we love the people we work with and do our best to help them understand the gospel, we will receive the joy and satis-faction that comes from being in tune with the Spirit of God. It is up to each individual to sincerely seek the Lord in prayer and receive a testimony of the gospel, but because of the love that we have for these people, as their prayers are answered, we will share in their happiness and our own joy will increase.

Index